Usborne A

100 Logic Puzzles

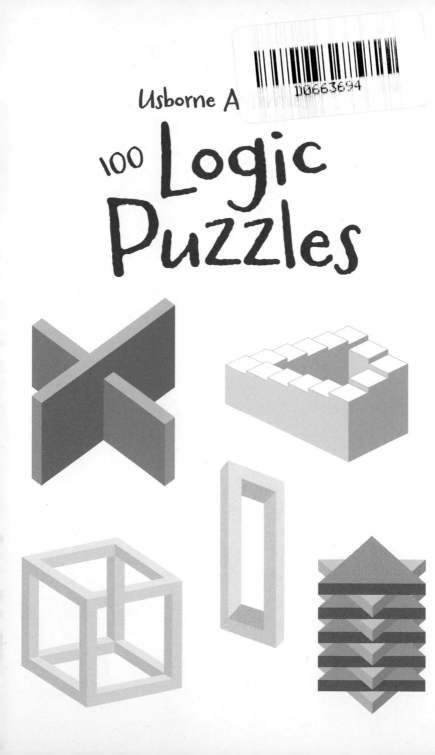

Logic tips

Logic puzzles are different from other puzzles. With most puzzles, you're told what to do, and the challenge lies in doing it. But with logic puzzles, the challenge lies in finding out what you're supposed to do in the first place. Once you know that, the rest is simple!

Here are some handy hints to help you along:

TIP 1. Word-based puzzles are sometimes designed to trick you. Look closely for clues in the details, and be careful of making assumptions.

TIP 2. If a puzzle involves a sequence of pictures, it can help to look for small details that you might not notice at first. If it's a number or letter sequence, try reading it aloud or writing it out in a straight line.

TIP 3. Sometimes, it's best to put a tricky puzzle aside and come back to it later. As you go through the book you'll pick up fresh ideas. But if you're really stuck, you can find explanations in the answer pages.

TIP 4. Finally, if you have an idea that makes you say, 'Why didn't I think of that before?' then it's almost certainly right. Logic puzzles are full of those eureka moments. Good luck!

Boat race

Nine boats set sail on a race across the bay. All but three of the boats spring a leak and turn back. How many boats make it to the other side?

Answer: ....

Lost stone

In the language of an ancient civilization:

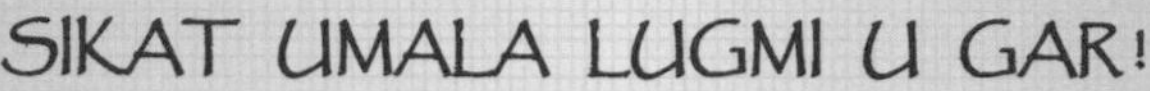
SIKAT UMALA LUGMI U GAR!

means 'The sacred stone is lost!'

GAR SHI LUGMI SIKAT!

means 'Find the lost stone!'

IRA GAR SIKAT U!

means 'The stone is ours!'

Draw a line to match each word with its meaning.

1. Stone	IRA
2. Lost	SIKAT
3. Ours	UMALA
4. Sacred	LUGMI

Odd one out

Which is the *odd one out*?

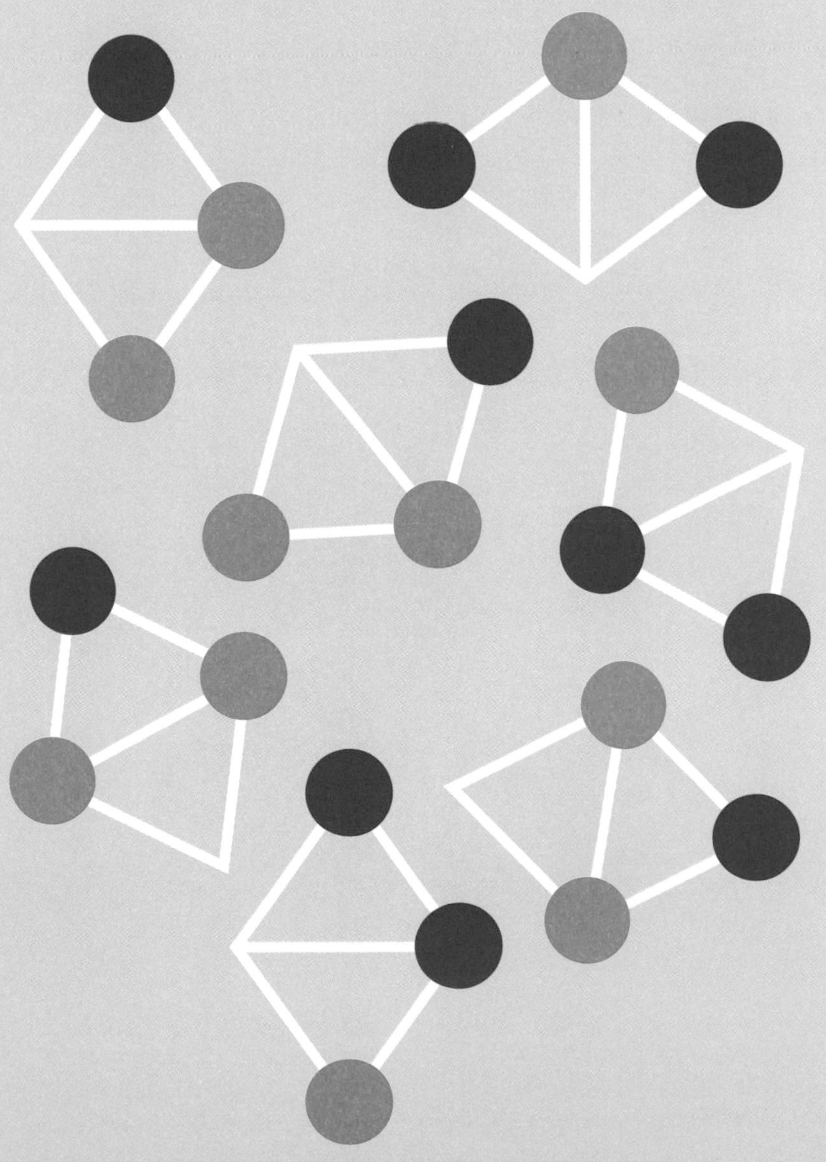

4

Alien weigh-in

On planet Zarf, weight is measured in grobbles.

1. If the baby alien weighs 20 grobbles plus half its own weight, how many grobbles does it weigh?

2. If the adult alien weighs the baby alien's weight, plus half its own weight, how many grobbles does it weigh?

Answers: ....

Tricky traffic

Find out what the cars on each road have in common, then choose the car that follows each pattern. Write their numbers in the empty circles.

6

Toy cube

This pattern can be folded to make *one of* the cubes below. Which *one*?

Dotty squares

Discover the pattern in the grid and draw the correct number of dots in the blank square.

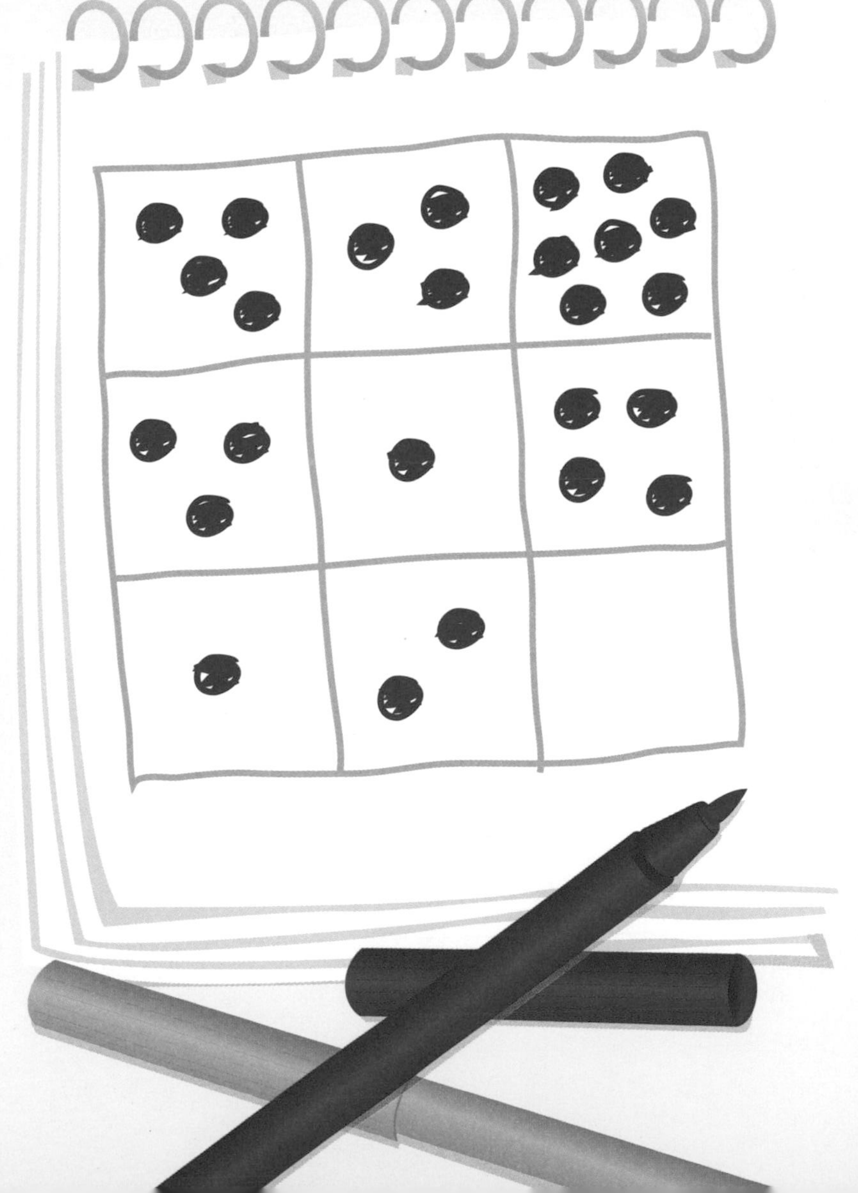

8

Who lives where?

There are three houses on this street. Two people live in each house. As you look at the houses...

- ...Mike lives directly to the right of Ray.
- ...Andy lives directly to the left of Mia.
- ...Mia lives directly to the left of Anna.
- ...Rose lives directly to the left of Mia.

Who lives where? Write each person's name under their house.

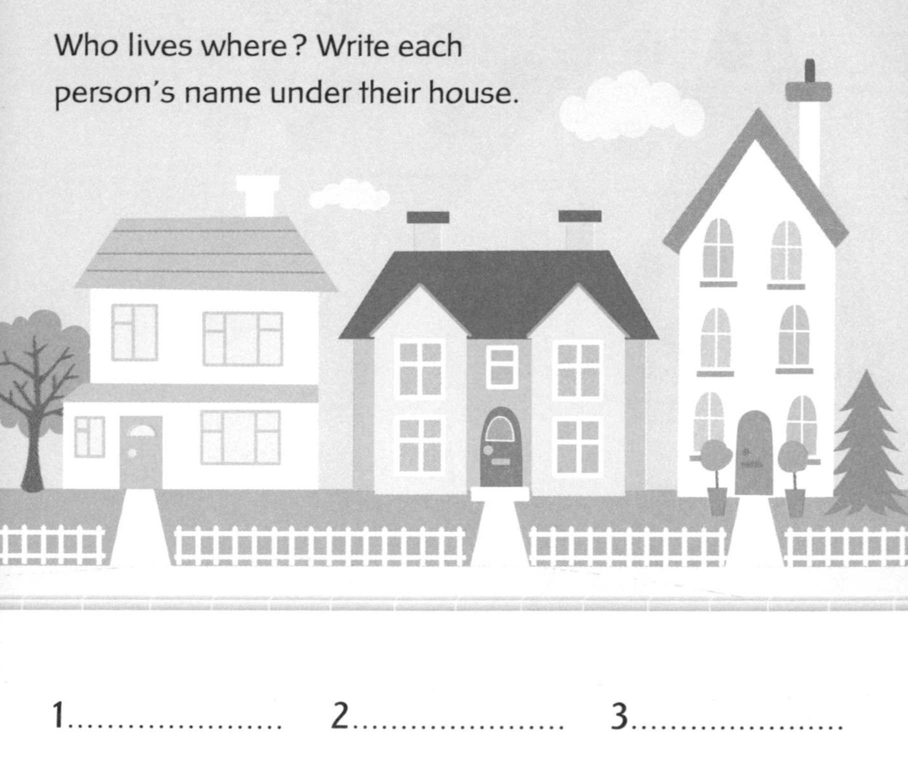

1...................... 2...................... 3......................

....

9

Bus driver riddle

A bus driver was heading down a street in Paris. He went past a stop sign without stopping. Then he turned left where there was a sign for 'NO LEFT TURN'. Finally, he went the wrong way down a one-way street. But after all this, no traffic laws had been broken. Why not?

Answer: ....

10

The jump

A girl jumped out of a 20 floor building, landed on her feet and walked away with no injuries. How?

Answer: ....

11

Racing positions

Five cars took part in a race.

- The purple car took third place.
- The yellow car came in before the purple car.
- The red car wasn't last, but it came after the yellow car.
- The green car wasn't first.
- The blue car came in before the yellow car.

Use this information to find out where each car finished and write their positions in the spaces below.

Pen puzzle

Draw this shape without lifting your pen from the page or going over any line that you've already made.

13

Shapes and numbers

Each number is connected to the shape above it. Find out how, then write the missing number under the hexagon.

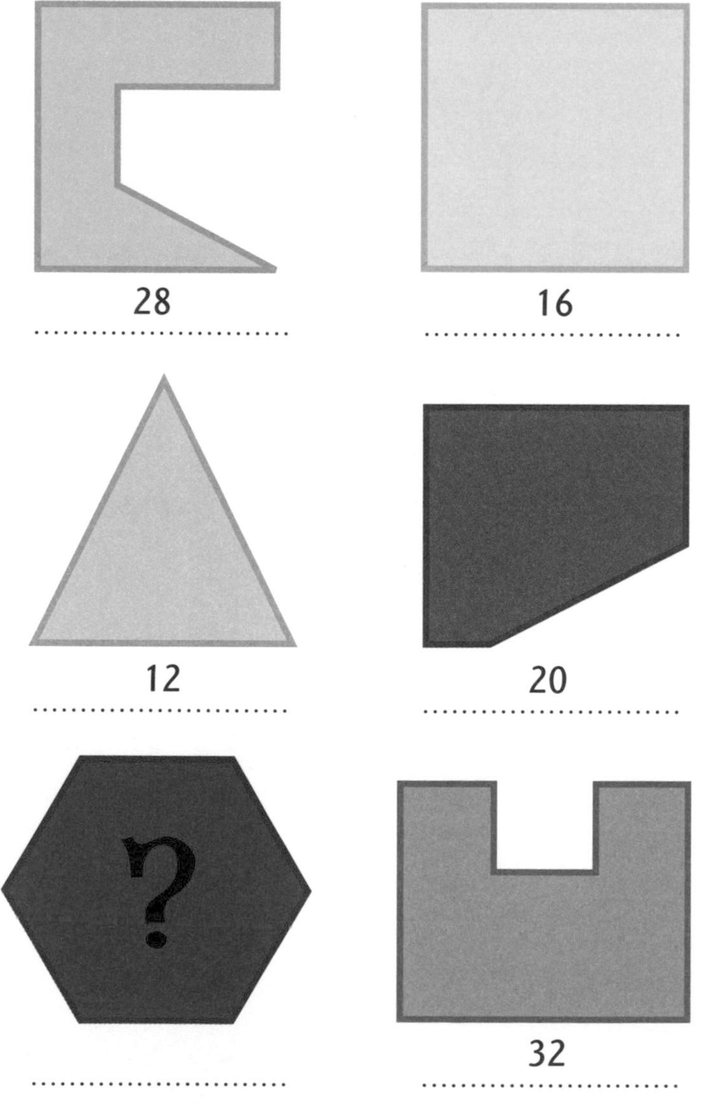

Which kitten?

When Joe's cat had kittens, his friends chose one each. There were four kittens:

- Sooty and Shadow were black with pink noses.
- Tiger and Rusty were orange with black noses.
- Sooty and Tiger were nervous.

- Zack didn't want a black kitten.
- Ellie wanted a kitten with a pink nose.
- Amy didn't want a kitten that was nervous.
- Rico had the kitten that neither Amy nor Zack wanted.

Fill in this chart with the name of each person's kitten.

Friend	Kitten
Zack	
Ellie	
Amy	
Rico	

15

Fishy puzzle

Make a copy of this fish, but draw it pointing upwards rather than left, by moving just two of its lines into different positions. The first two lines have been done for you.

Odd pattern out

Which is the *odd one out*?

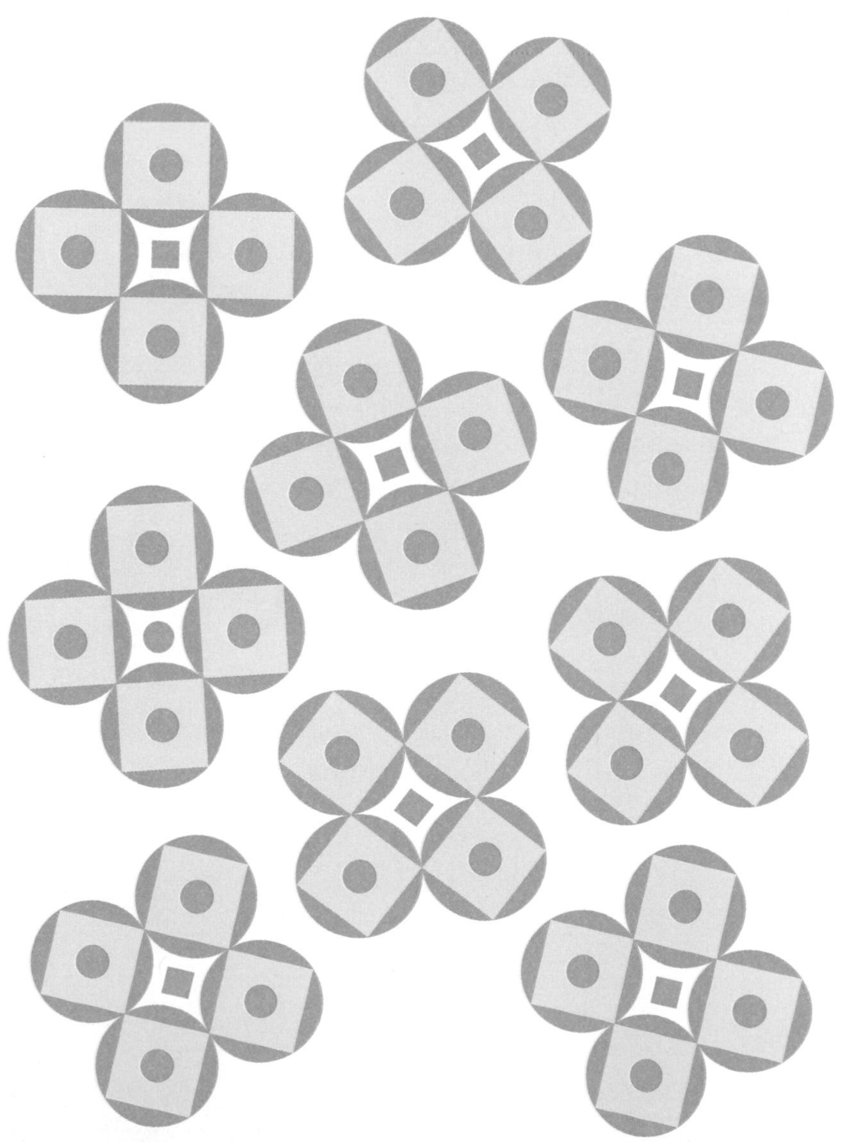

Dog toys

Three dog owners are playing with their dogs in the park, and each owner has brought a different toy. Follow the clues to find out who owns which dog, and which toy they are playing with. Draw a ✓ in the correct boxes for each person.

Clues:

1. Ali is not playing with the ball.

2. Riz does not own Rex.

3. The person who owns Jojo is playing with the ball.

4. Pat is playing with the bone.

5. The person who is playing with the stick does not own Spot.

	Jojo	Rex	Spot	Bone	Ball	Stick
Ali						
Pat						
Riz						

Pencil puzzle

18

Using a pen, cross out six pencils to make ten.

The wise son

19

A dying king wants to leave his kingdom to the wiser of his two sons. He takes them outside for a horse race, but tells them the son whose horse finishes LAST will inherit the realm. The younger son immediately jumps on a horse and rides it over the finish line at top speed. The king leaves him the kingdom. Why?

Puzzle time

Which two clocks are the *odd ones out*?

Dots on dice

These four dice show all the numbers that are visible if you turn a dice around while keeping the '6' on top. Look at them carefully and fill in the dots on the net below.

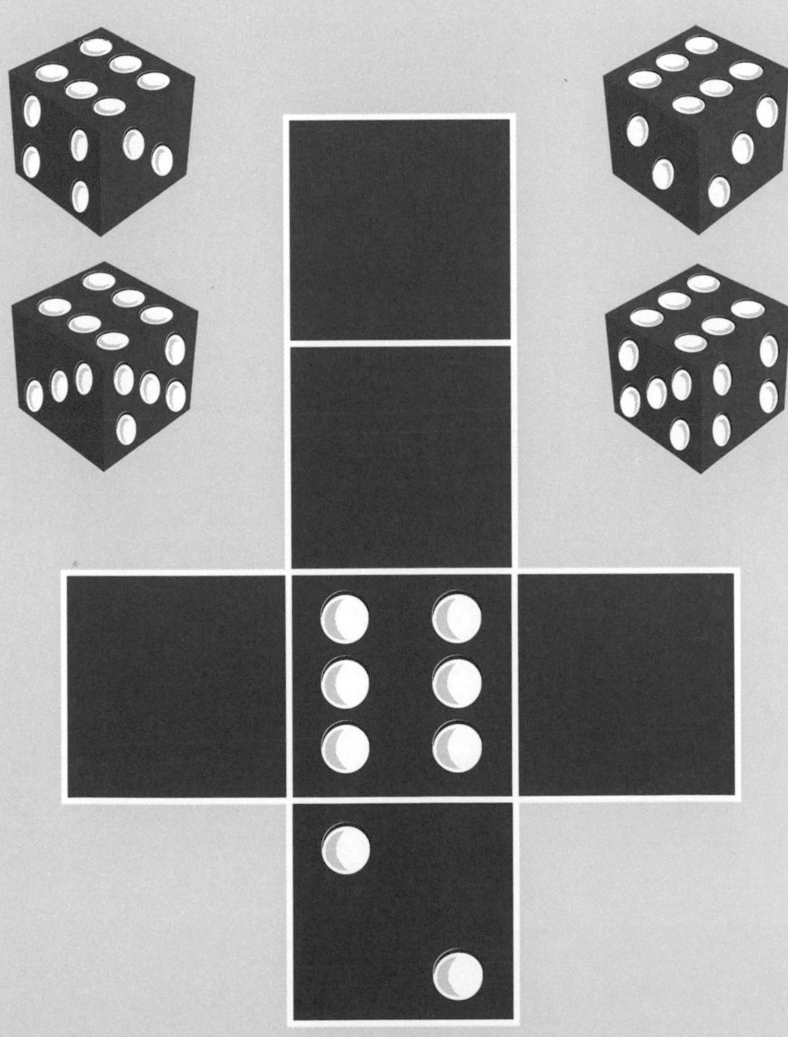

Sudoku

This grid is made up of nine blocks, each containing nine squares. Fill in the blank squares so that each block contains all the digits 1 to 9. Each digit can only appear once in a row, column or block.

		1	2		3	8		
	4			5			2	
5		7				1		6
4			7		1			5
	5			3			7	
3			5		2			9
2		6				7		3
	1			2			6	
		5	8		7	2		

Bell ringer

To strike the bell, should you turn the handle around to the left or right?

Answer: ....

Breakfast code

Each letter represents a different type of food. Find out what's what, then draw the right items on the empty plate.

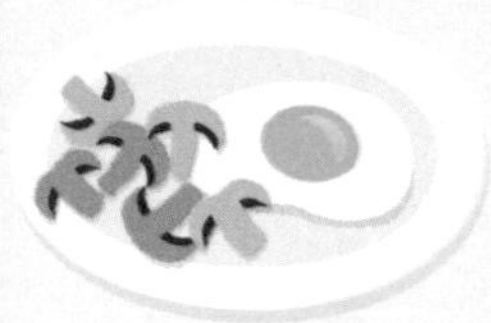

A B

G H

I H

D G

A C

D F

Mission to Mars

A rocket blasts off for Mars. By the end of its first week in space, the rocket has left the Earth far behind and is getting faster all the time. In fact, its distance from Earth doubles each week.

If the rocket reaches Mars in week 12, in which week was it halfway there?

a) week 2

b) week 6

c) week 11

Not knots

Only one of these ropes would make a knot if you pulled both ends. Which one?

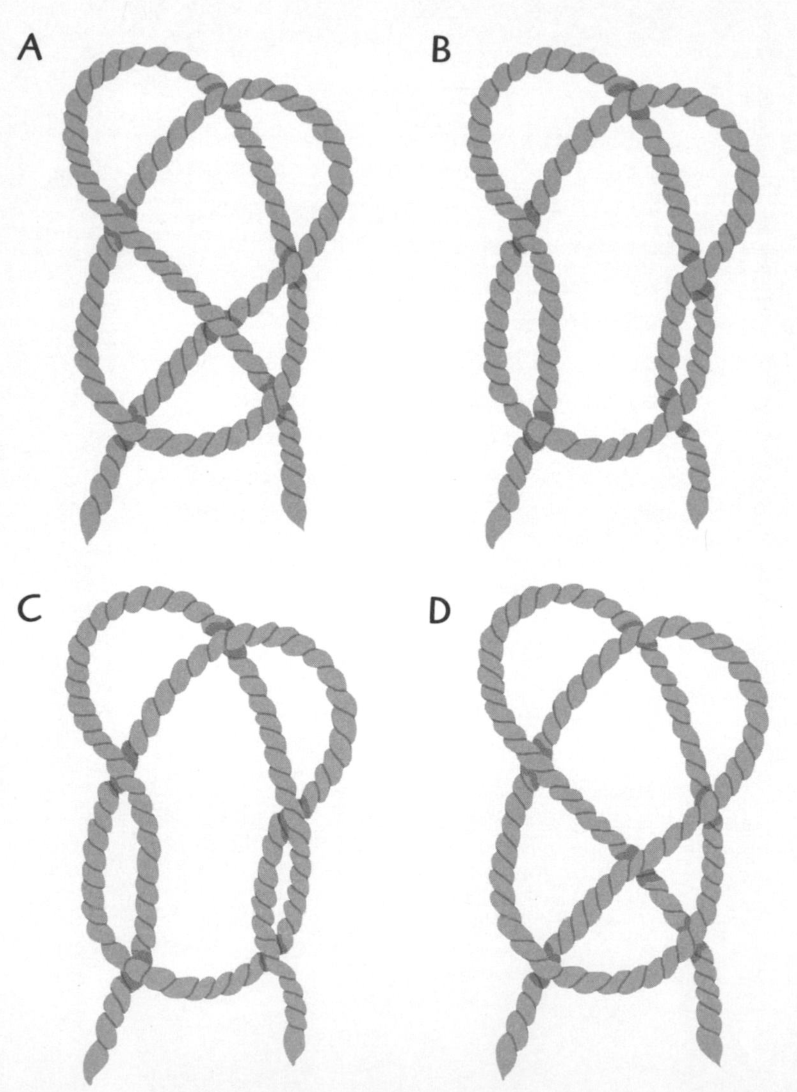

Genie's riddle

A sly genie is called from his lamp and says: "I will grant you three wishes, young master, but only if you answer my riddle. There are three rooms set before you, and you must enter one. The first is filled with raging fire, the second with bloodthirsty bandits, the third is filled with lions that haven't eaten in three years. Think carefully, my eager daredevil. Which room should you choose?"

Answer: ....

28

Right rectangle

Find out the relationship between the rectangles in row 1, then use the same logic to discover which rectangle completes row 2.

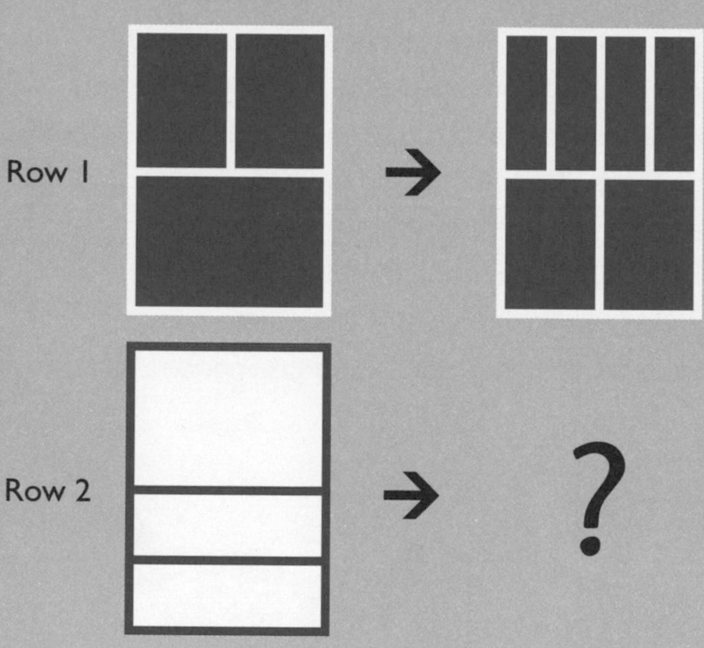

Circle the right answer.

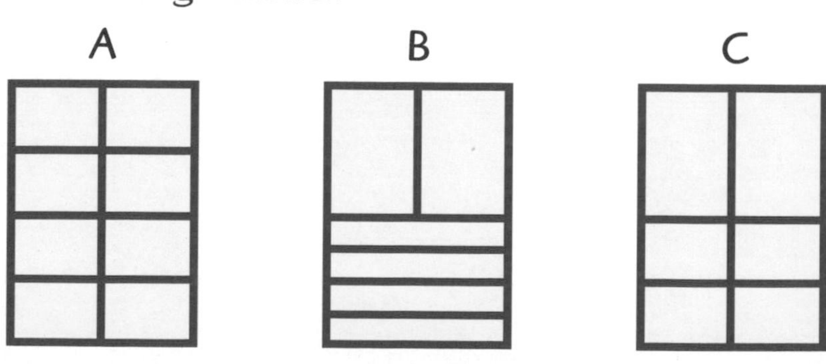

Sequence challenge

Look at the sequence below, and find out what links each line with the one directly above. Then write the next line in the space provided.

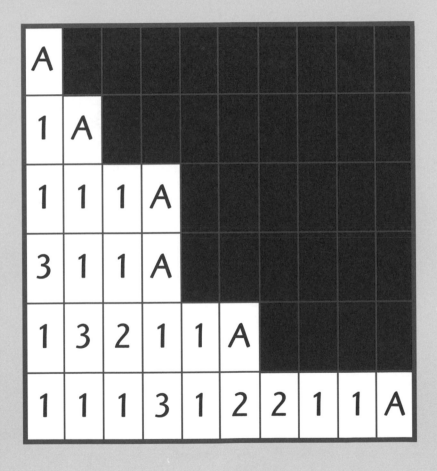

A									
1	A								
1	1	1	A						
3	1	1	A						
1	3	2	1	1	A				
1	1	1	3	1	2	2	1	1	A

Answer: ....

Follow the cogs

If the green cog at the top turns around to the right, which way will the red cog at the bottom turn? Use a pen to find out by tracing the movement of each cog.

Answer: ....

Fish in a bowl

Find out the relationship between the bowls in row 1, then use the same logic to discover which bowl completes row 2.

Circle the right answer.

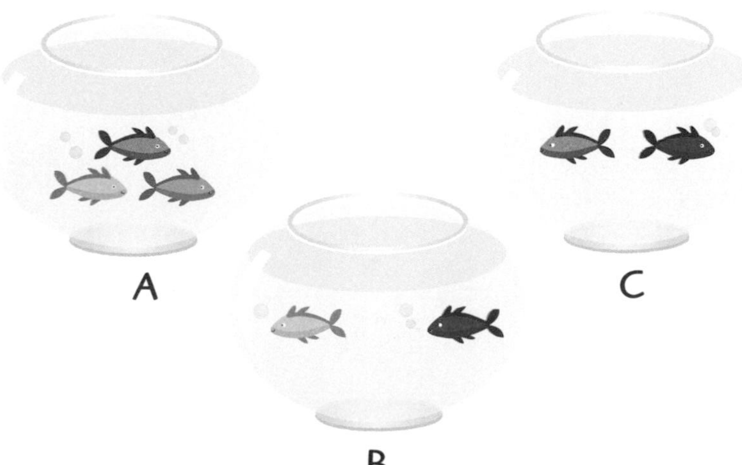

Hen names

Look carefully at the picture and match each hen to its name.

Henny	Po	Maisie
....	....	....
Meg	**Gina**	**Eggwina**
....	....	....

1

2

3

4

5

6

Block prints

If this block is turned on its side so the dotted lines are face down, which print will it make?

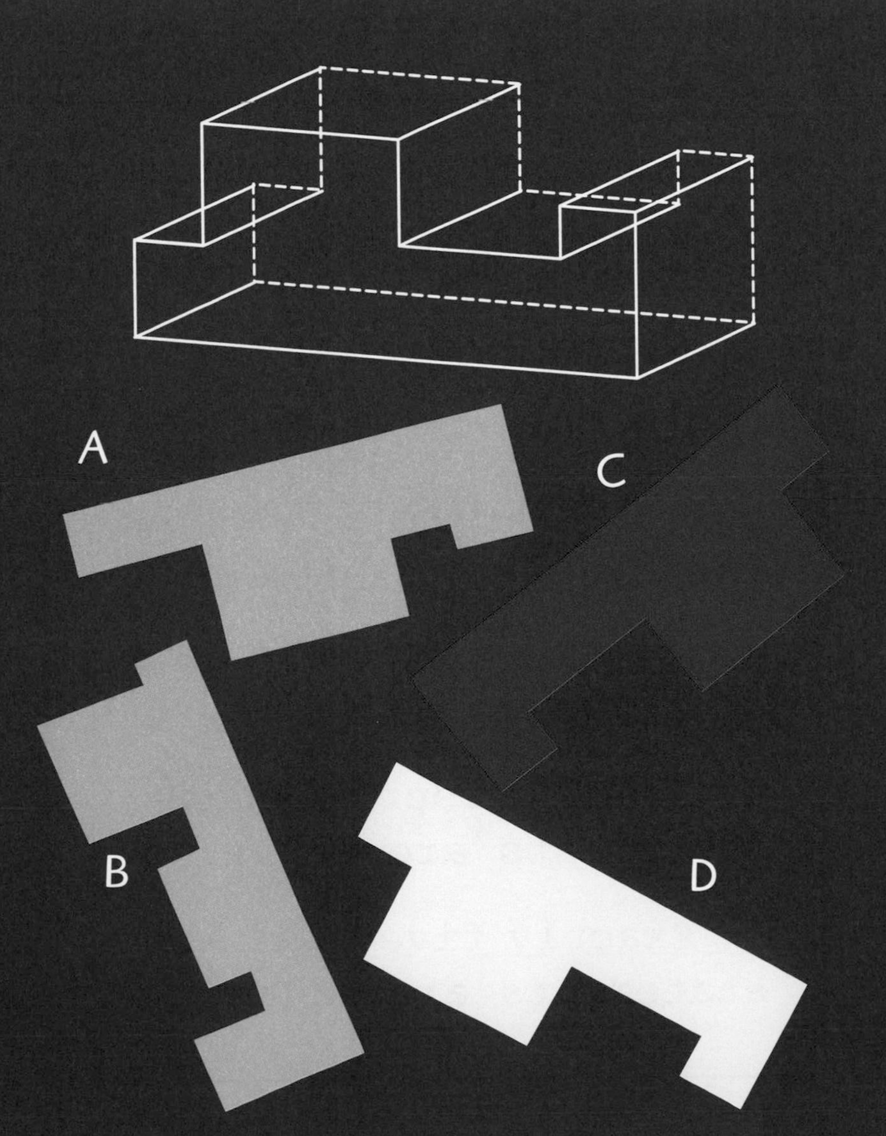

Detective school

Priya wants to be a detective, so her dad sets her a question to test her logic skills. She's given five statements and told only one of them is true. Which one?

CASE 3

1. Exactly one of these statements is false.

2. Exactly two of these statements are false.

3. Exactly three of these statements are false.

4. Exactly four of these statements are false.

5. Exactly five of these statements are false.

Cake gobbler

What comes next: A, B or C?

1

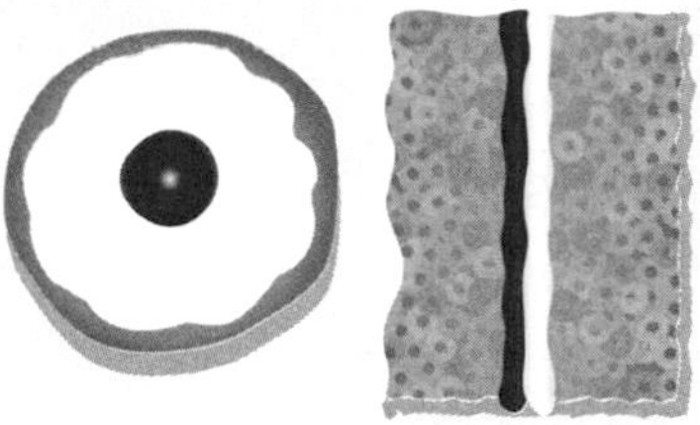

2

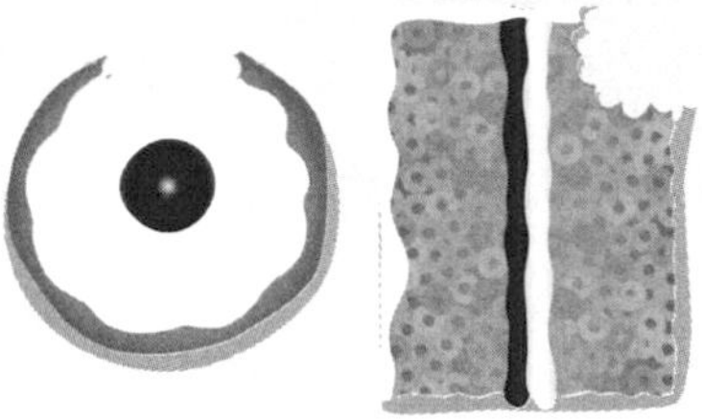

3

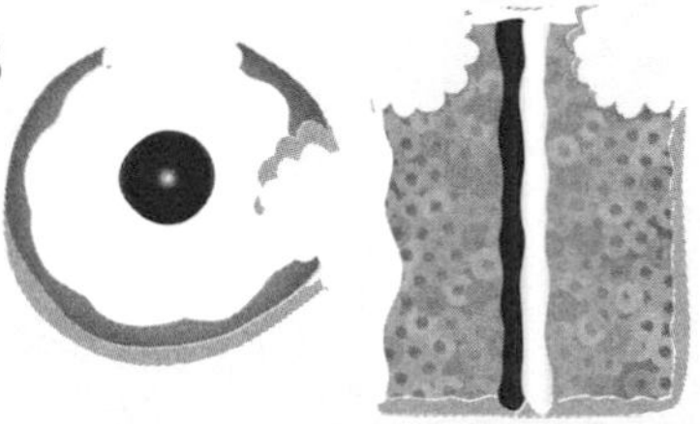

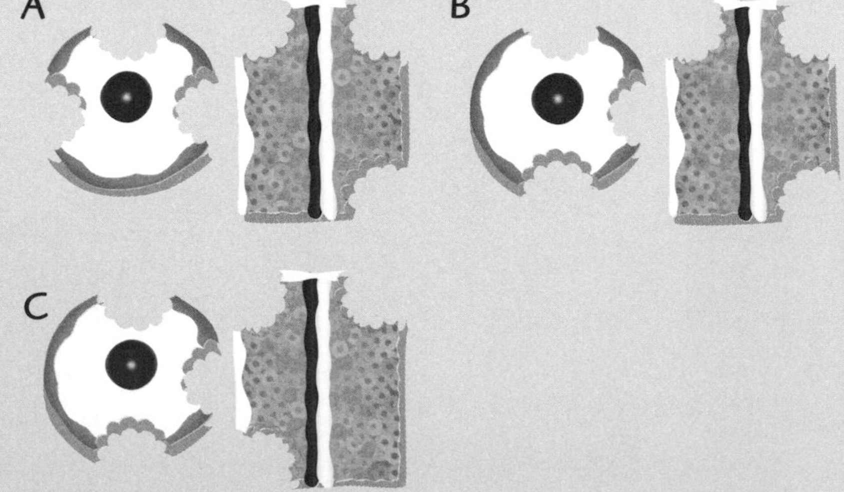

A

B

C

Wild West

Three cowboys ride into Dodge City. Each cowboy arrives on a different day and has a different errand. Follow the clues on the opposite page to match the cowboy with their horse, and find out when each arrived and where they went. Fill in your answers on the chart below.

Day	Cowboy	Horse	Errand
Thursday			
Friday			
Saturday			

1. Jesse rode in some time after another cowboy had been to buy a saddle.
2. Betsy carried her owner into town on Thursday.
3. Butch did not go to the dentist.
4. Billy owns Red Lady, and arrived later in the week than the cowboy who was collecting a debt.
5. Dusty was not ridden into town on Saturday.

You can use the chart below to keep track of the facts.

	Billy	Butch	Jesse	Dusty	Betsy	Red Lady	Debt	Dentist	Saddle
Thursday									
Friday									
Saturday									
Debt									
Dentist									
Saddle									
Dusty									
Betsy									
Red Lady									

Pencils and pens

Circle the item that is...

1. ...two to the left of the item that's six to the right of the item that's one to the left of the item that's four to the right of the item that's directly to the left of the black pen.

2. ...two to the left of the item that's six to the left of the item that's two to the right of the item that's three to the right of the item that's directly to the left of the blue pen?

Shooting stars

Which two of these pictures can be rotated so they match each other exactly?

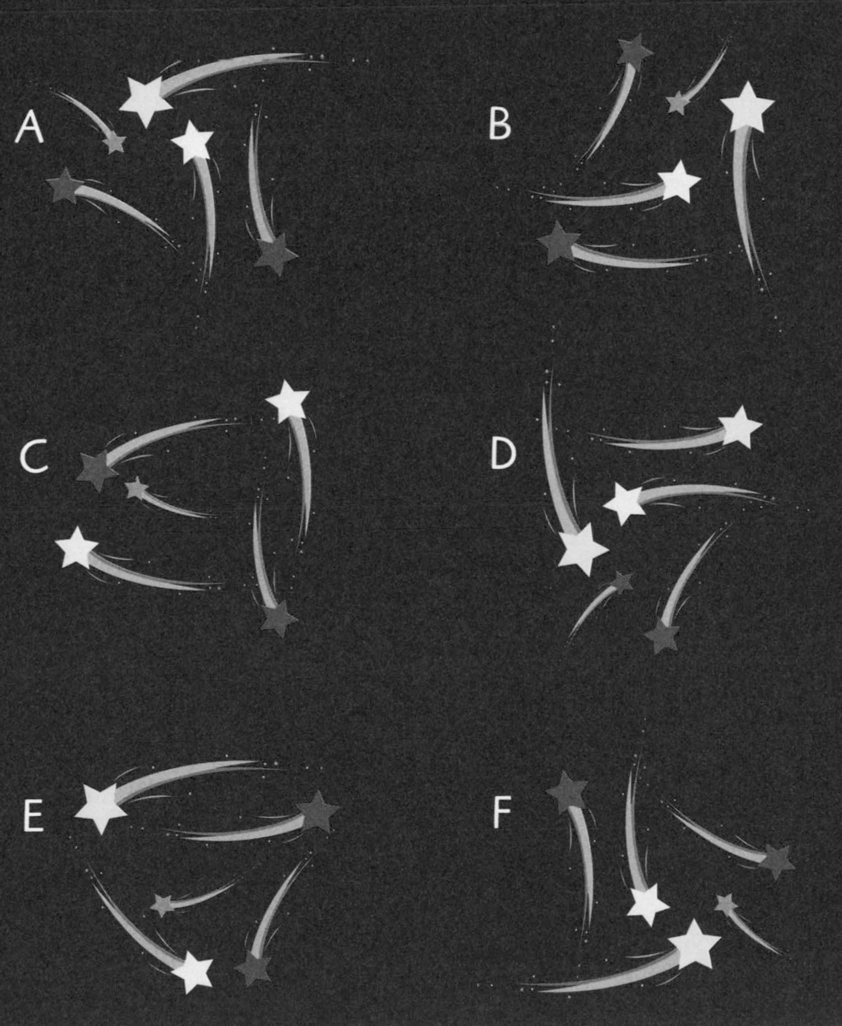

Answer: ....

Cuckoo clock

If this clock takes two seconds to strike two o'clock, how long will it take to strike three o'clock?

Answer: ....

Murder mystery

Four friends are watching a murder mystery movie, set in the criminal underworld.

- Sam thinks the corrupt cop is the murderer.
- Anil is sure that the victim's wife did it.
- Dalia thinks it's either the gangster or the cop.
- Lou is certain that the murderer is the gangster.

If only one of the friends is right, which character is the murderer? Write your answer below.

Answer: ....

41

Patchwork pattern

Discover the pattern that links the grids, then mark with an X the position of the orange square in grid 6.

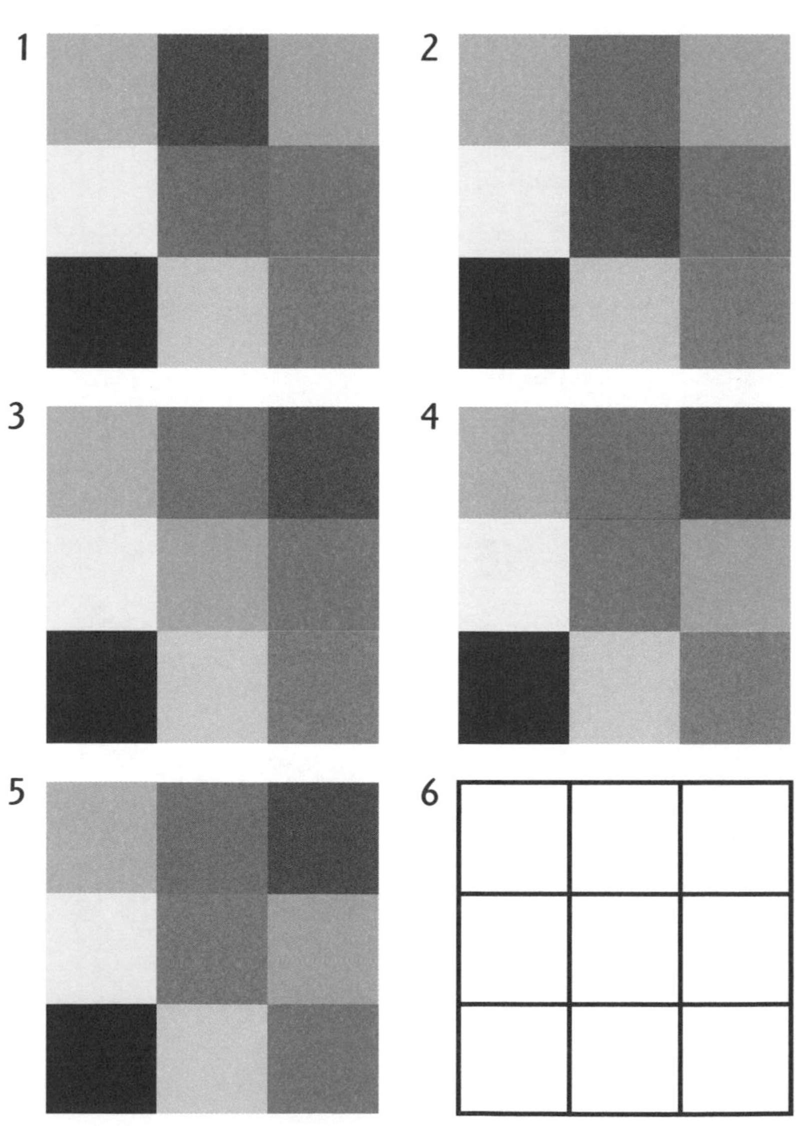

Prism picker

Which three shapes could fold up to make the hexagonal prism in the middle?

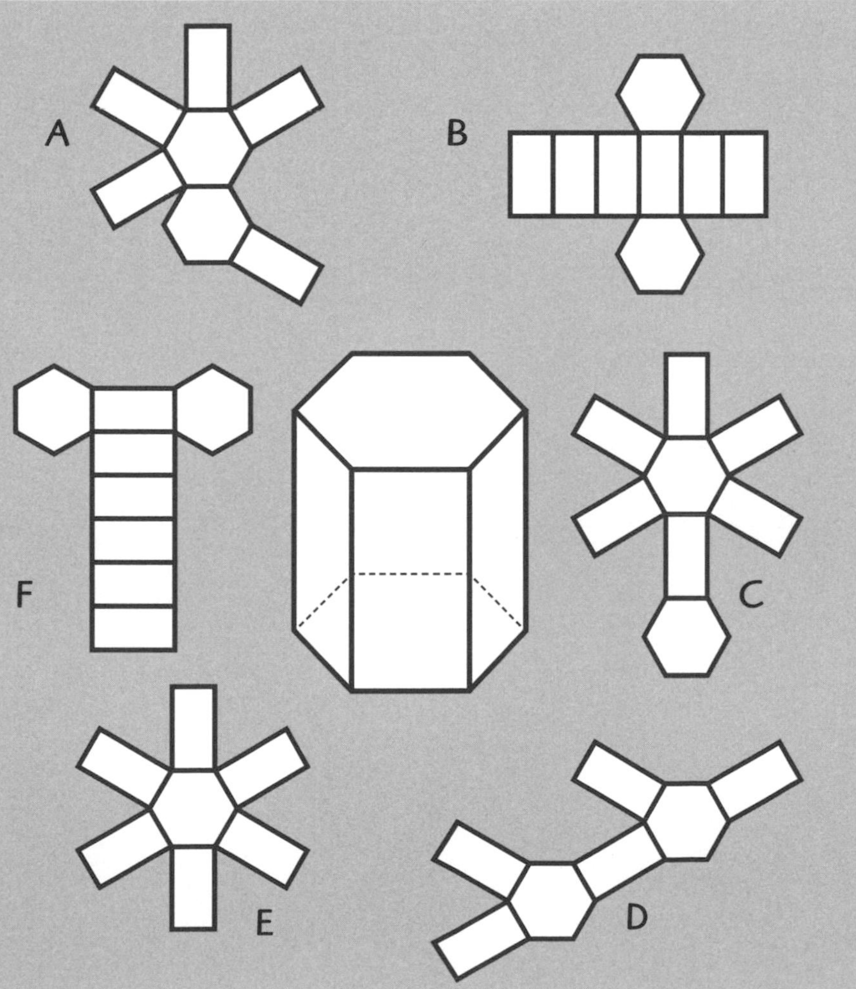

Answer: ....

Postage puzzle

The prices are missing from some of these stamps. Find out how they're numbered and fill in the gaps.

Puzzling print

Only one of the prints below can be made with this potato. Which one?

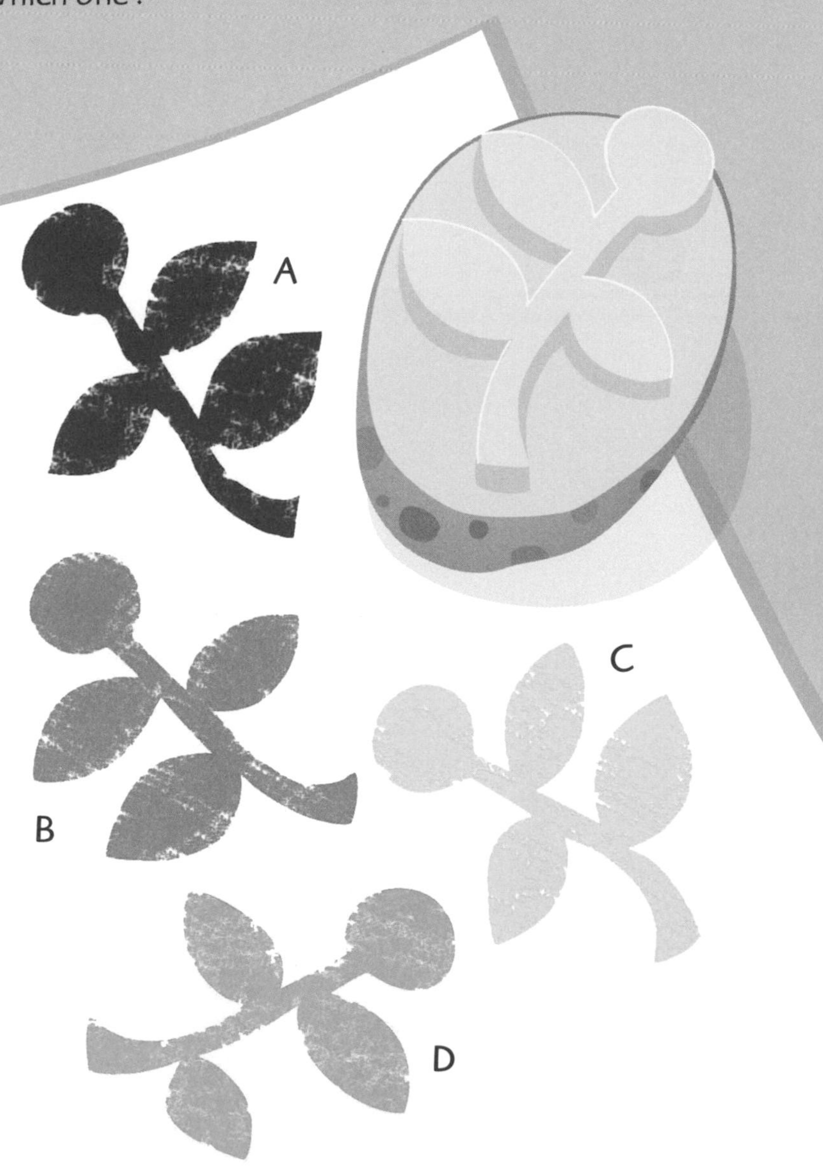

45

See-saw scales

The triangle, circle and square each weigh a different amount. The first two scales balance, but the bottom ones don't. Draw a single shape on the left side of the bottom scales that would make them balance.

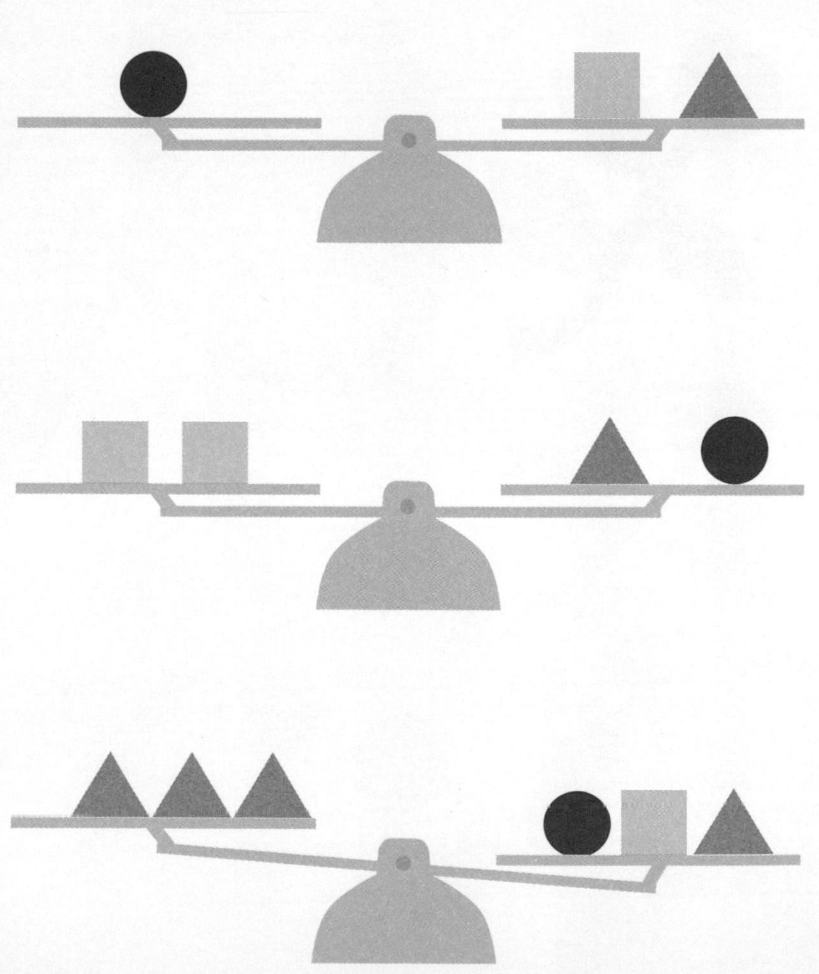

46

Jester's riddle

A jester stands on his head and says: "Everyone calls me a fool, but no one can answer my riddle! Can you? A warty old man has a gaggle of daughters. They're all blonde but two, all brunette but two, and all redheaded but two. How many daughters does the old man have?"

Answer: ....

47

Near miss

Blackberry the rabbit is wandering along a train track, when a train comes speeding towards him. Instead of leaping straight off the track, he bounds along for five seconds then leaps out of the way just in time. Why doesn't he leap off right away?

Answer: ....

....

Shape shifter

Find out the pattern to uncover what comes next.

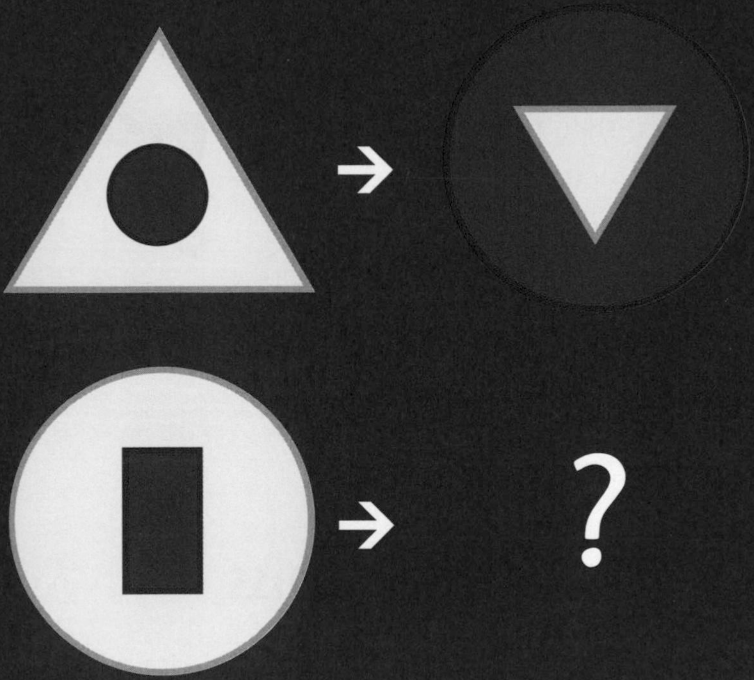

→

→ ?

Circle the right answer.

A

B

C

Roman riddle

A man wants to enter the temple but has forgotten the password, so he hides behind a pillar and listens carefully. Soon, another man walks up. The guard looks down at him and says in a gruff voice: "twelve". The man replies "six" and is let in. Then a woman walks up and the guard says "six". She replies "three" and is let in. The man thinks he's heard enough and strides up to the door. The guard says "ten", he says "five", but the guard turns him away. What should he have said?

a) two b) three c) four

Cryptic grid

See if you can complete this grid by drawing in the missing symbols.

Symbol sudoku

This grid is made up of nine blocks, each containing nine squares. Fill in the blank squares so that each of the nine blocks contains all the symbols at the bottom of this page. Each symbol can only appear once in a row, column or block.

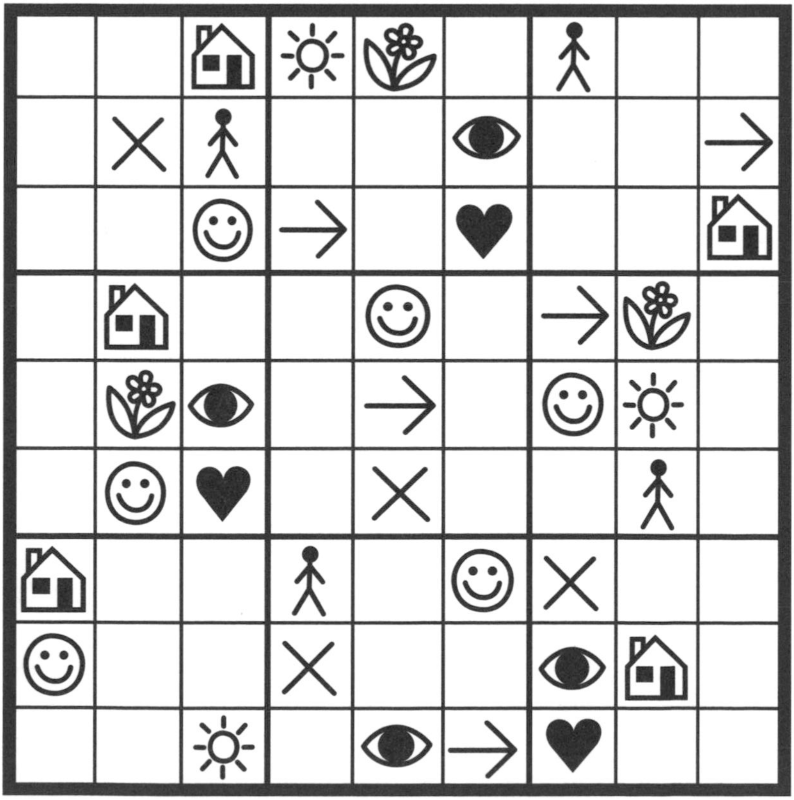

Pattern puzzler

Find the connection between each gift wrap and its tag, then look at the options below and choose the correct tag for the fourth gift wrap.

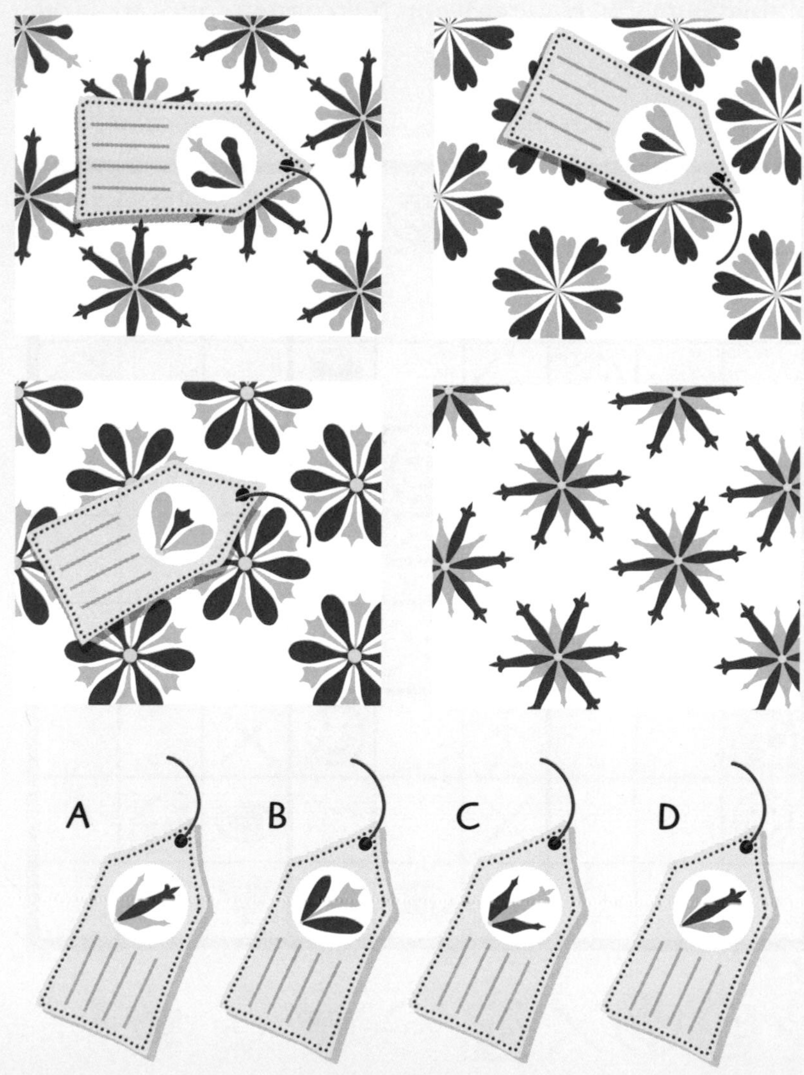

Tom the cat

Tom the cat has led an eventful life. He spent $\frac{1}{4}$ of it in a peasant's cottage with little food, $\frac{1}{8}$ of it working as a ship's cat, and $\frac{1}{2}$ of it catching rats in a sultan's palace. If he's been living with the mayor of London for the past 2 years, how long did he spend doing each thing?

.... years living in a peasant's house.

.... years working as a ship's cat.

.... years catching rats for the sultan.

Tom is .... years old.

Detective work

In each set of statements, underline the **two** which prove that:

1. A tiger has escaped from the zoo.

a. The tiger enclosure in the zoo is empty.
b. The zoo's only tiger has one ear.
c. The zoo has been closed for the day.
d. There's a one-eared tiger loose in the park.
e. The zoo keepers are all panicking.

2. Edward is a pirate.

a. Edward is a sailor on the Black Dragon.
b. Edward has a parrot.
c. The Black Dragon has red sails.
d. Edward wears an eye patch.
e. The sailors on the Black Dragon steal treasure.

3. The prince fought a giant dragon.

a. The dragon is dead.
b. The prince said he killed the dragon.
c. There's blue blood on the prince's sword and tunic.
d. The prince is known for being very brave.
e. The giant dragon has blue blood.

Seaside puzzle

Someone has left a puzzle in the sand. Using the numbers 3 to 6, see if you can fill in the empty squares so that none of the numbers sits in numerical order. For example, 3 couldn't be placed directly above, below or beside 2.

Choose carefully

A girl finds two identical doors at the end of a secret corridor. Behind one door there are riches beyond her wildest dreams; behind the other there's a pair of sweaty boots. There is a guard at each door. One always tells the truth, and the other always lies, but she doesn't know which is which. Before she picks a door, the girl can choose one guard and ask him one question.

What question should she ask to find the treasure?

Hint: Think of a question that makes the honest guard reply with a lie. Then the reply is a lie whichever guard you ask.

Answer: ....

....

Testing tubes

Boris heats two test tubes, each half-filled with chemical mixture. After five minutes, the liquid doubles in volume and fills each tube. He splits the liquid between four test tubes, heats it for another five minutes and it doubles again. Then he splits it between eight tubes, and so on.

In four hours he makes enough mixture to fill a large barrel. How long would it take if he only started out with one half-filled test tube?

a) 4 hrs and 5 mins   b) 4 hrs and 30 mins   c) 8 hrs

Art club

Find out what links all the pictures in this art club display, then choose from the options below and draw the correct design on the blank page.

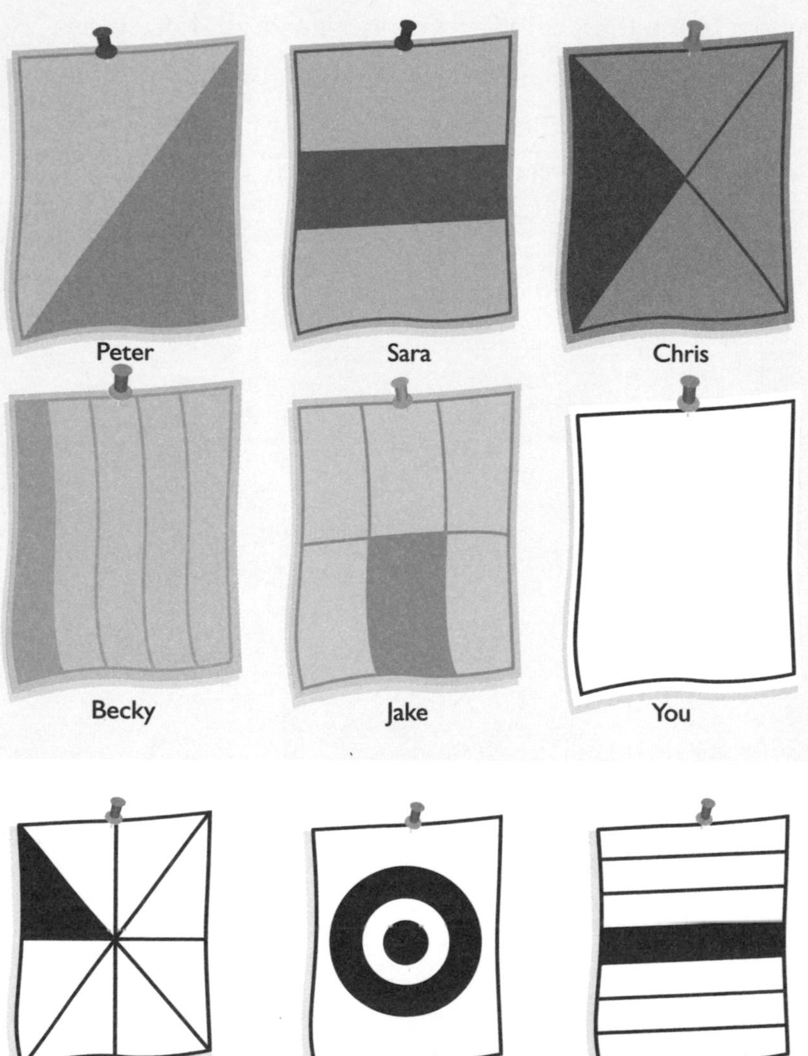

Hat puzzler

A man stands on one side of a solid brick wall, and three men line up, one behind the other, facing the other side. The man at the back sees both men in front of him. The man in the middle sees only the man in front of him. The man in front sees only the wall.

They close their eyes while a hat is placed on each of their heads. They're told two are yellow and two are blue. Then they're asked: "In 30 seconds, can any of you say which hat you're wearing?" They can't move, or talk to each other. Which is the only man who can answer the question?

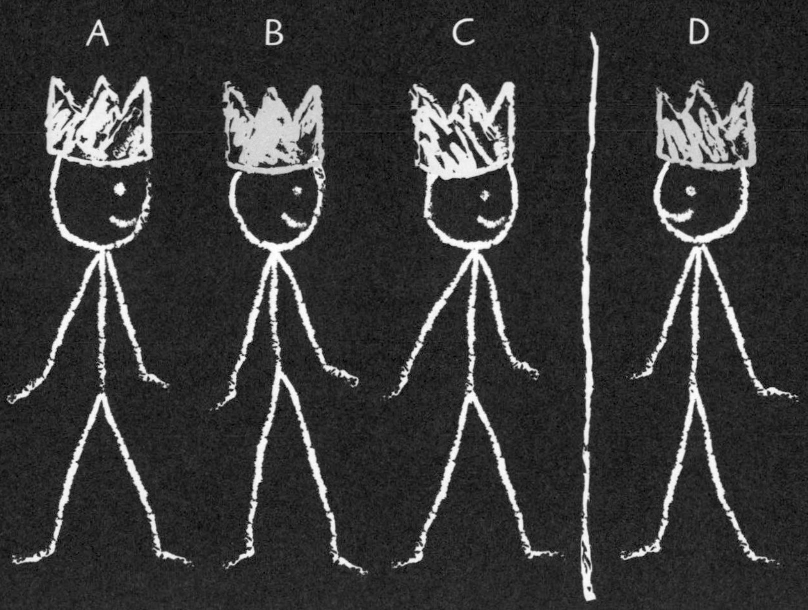

Hint: The man who can answer needs to think about what one of the other men must be seeing.

Answer: ....

Lollipop pick

Which row comes next, A *or* B?

Pattern streamers

Find out the sequence then draw the next two patterns below.

Planes puzzle

Four planes take off from the same airport at the same time.

- The first plane returns to the airport once a day.
- The second plane returns every other day.
- The third plane returns every three days.
- The fourth plane returns every four days.

If they take off on Day 1, which is the next day when all four planes are due back in the airport together?

Answer: ....

Faulty calculator

The numbers and symbols on the screens below are made up of segments. Correct each calculation in a different way, by moving just one segment to anywhere in the line.

6+4=4

6+4=4

6+4=4

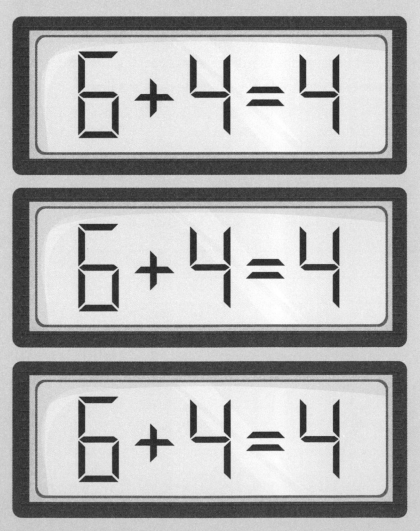

River crossing

A farmer stands on one side of a river with a fox, a rabbit and a bunch of carrots. She needs to take them across, but can only carry one thing at a time.

If she leaves the fox and rabbit alone together, the fox will eat the rabbit. If she leaves the rabbit and carrots together, the rabbit will eat the carrots. Complete the chart below to find out how she can take them to the other side in the fewest number of crossings.

Left shore	On the boat	Right shore
F,R,C		
F,C	R	
F,C		R
C	F	R

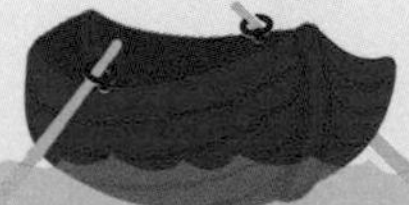

Sudoku

This grid is made up of nine blocks, each containing nine squares. Fill in the blank squares so that each block contains all the digits 1 to 9. Each digit can only appear once in a row, column or block.

		9	4		6	5		
	2			3			6	
1		5				7		3
3			8		4			1
	1			5			8	
2			3		9			5
4		3				8		9
	9			4			3	
		1	5		3	4		

Paperboy puzzle

A paperboy's route goes from orange door, to red door, to purple door, to yellow door. If he continues his route with this pattern, what's the number of the house he'll deliver to next?

Answer: ....

Cube finder

This pattern can be folded to make *only one* of the cubes below. Which *one*?

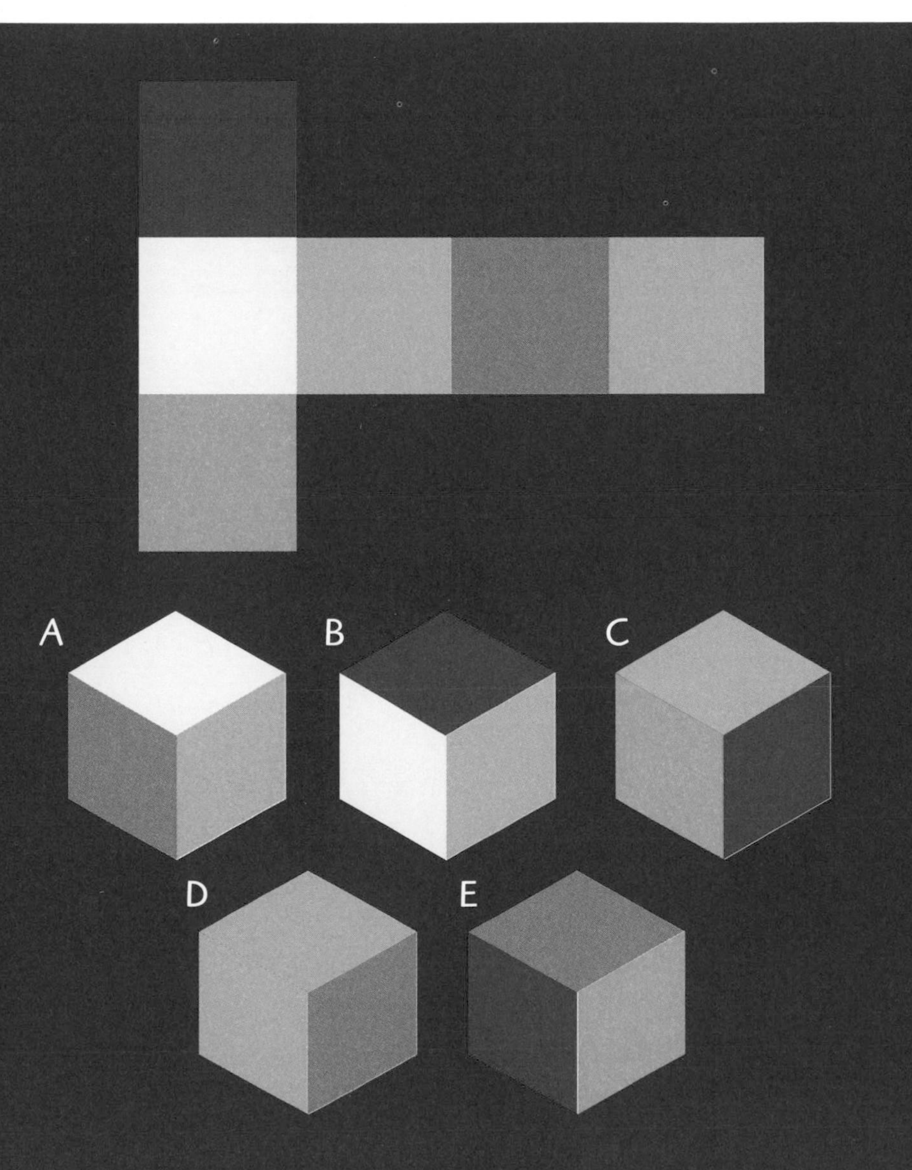

68

Wrong total

Zina and six of her friends are visiting Italy. They all go into a café and choose the same ice cream. The price comes to 24 euros and Zina knows it is wrong, even though she can't remember how much each ice cream cost. Why is this?

Answer: ....

69

Age puzzler

On Laura's 5th birthday, her mother was 35. On her 15th birthday, her mother was 3 times her age. How old is Laura now that her mother is only twice her age?

Answer: ....

Tricky triangles

The number in the middle of each triangle is made by doing a calculation with the numbers in each corner. The calculation is the same for all the triangles. Write the missing numbers on the bottom two triangles.

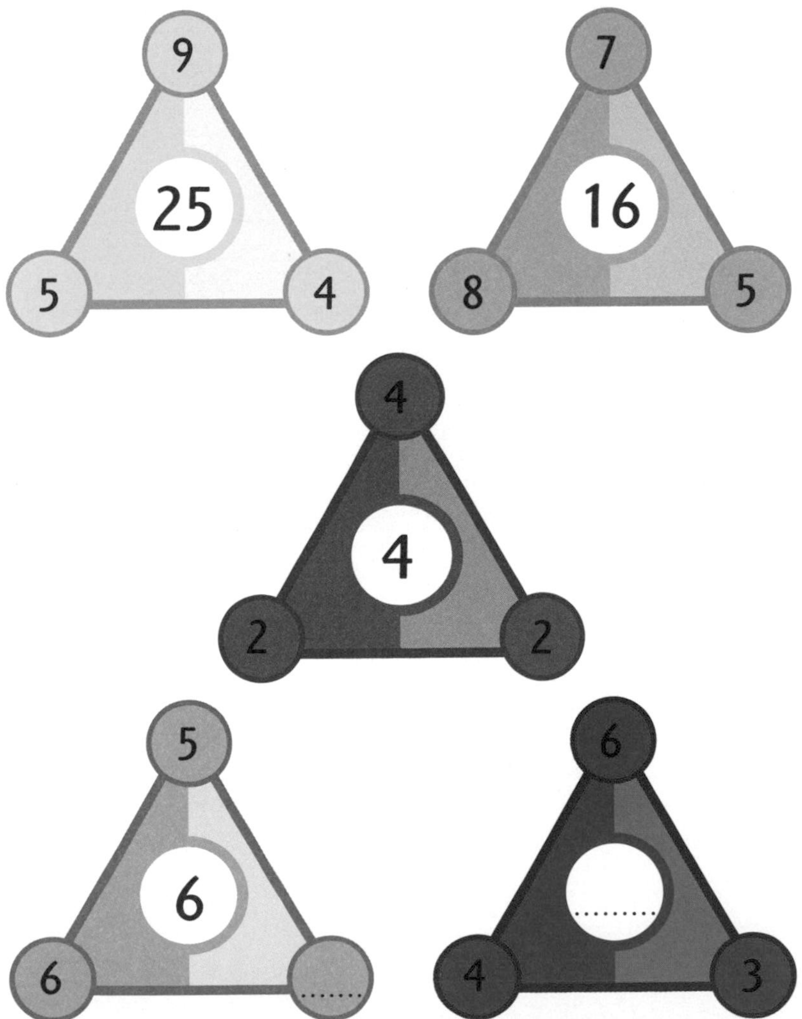

In the bay

Three boats are docked at a jetty. Following the clues on the opposite page, can you find out the owner of each boat, the number on its sail and its age?

Name	Owner	Number	Age
Salt Spray			
Merrimack			
Crab's Claw			

1. The boat with 109 on its sail is one year older than the Crab's Claw, which is owned by Seb.

2. The owner of the boat that is 3 years old isn't Mick, who has a boat numbered 364.

3. The Salt Spray isn't owned by Joss.

4. The Merrimack is 3 years old.

You can use the chart below to keep track of the facts.

	109	238	364	Joss	Seb	Mick	1 year	2 years	3 years
Salt Spray									
Merrimack									
Crab's Claw									
1 year									
2 years									
3 years									
Joss									
Seb									
Mick									

What's the time?

Look at the clocks to find out what time the green clock should show, then draw its hands in the correct position.

Bird's eye view

Look carefully at the shapes on the board below. Which image would they make if you were looking at them from directly above?

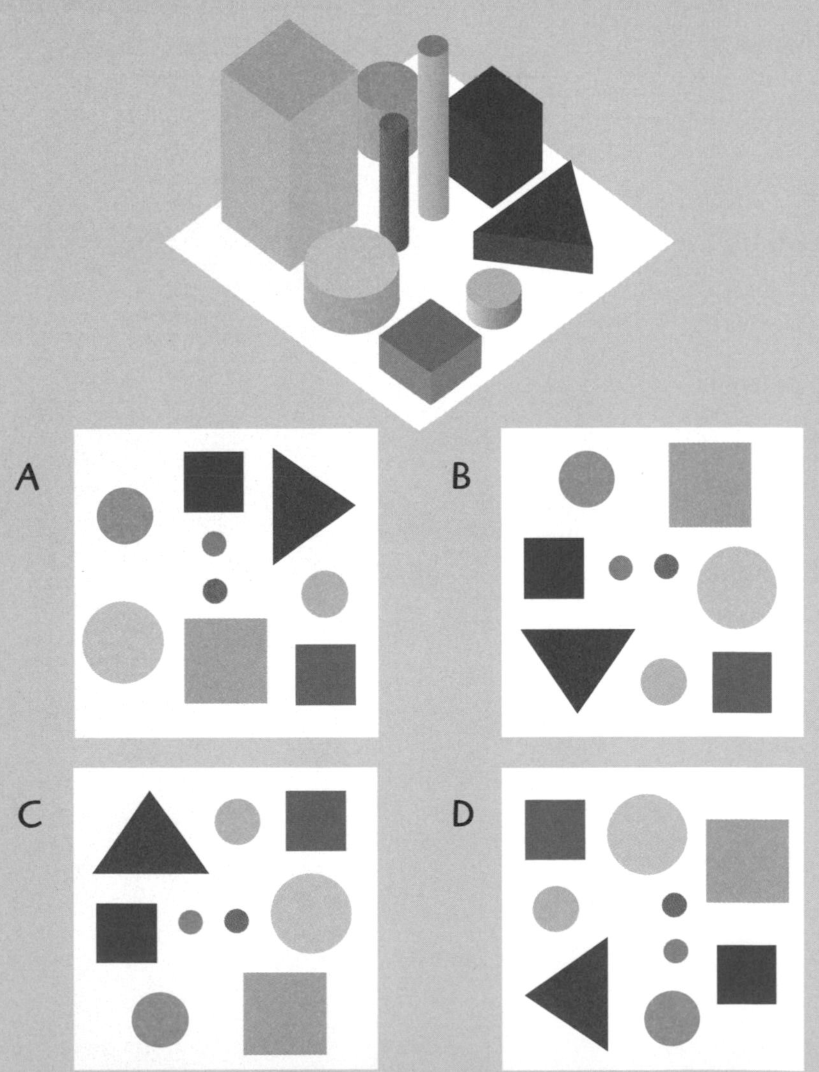

Short puzzles

1. What is the next letter in this sequence?

O T T F F S S ?

Answer: ....

2. If a sharp prod can be spelled POKE, and a cape can be spelled CLOAK, how do you spell the white of an egg?

Answer: ....

3. Mary's mother has four children. The first child is called April, the second is called May and the third is called June. What's the name of the fourth child?

Answer: ....

4. At midnight it is raining hard. What are the chances of it being sunny in 72 hours' time, if 0% is no chance, and 100% is a cast-iron certainty?

Answer: ....%

Parrot in a cage

This parrot and cage cost 50 silver pieces. If the parrot costs 40 silver pieces more than the cage, how much does each of them cost? Write your answers on the card below.

For sale
Cage: .... silver pieces
Parrot: .... silver pieces

Jumbo jumble

There are three pairs of souvenir elephants. The elephants in each pair weigh the same, but one pair is heavier than the other two. You have some balance scales, but you can only use them once. How do you find out which pair of elephants is heaviest?

Impossible shapes

Three of the shapes below can be drawn on paper, but cannot exist in real life. Which are they?

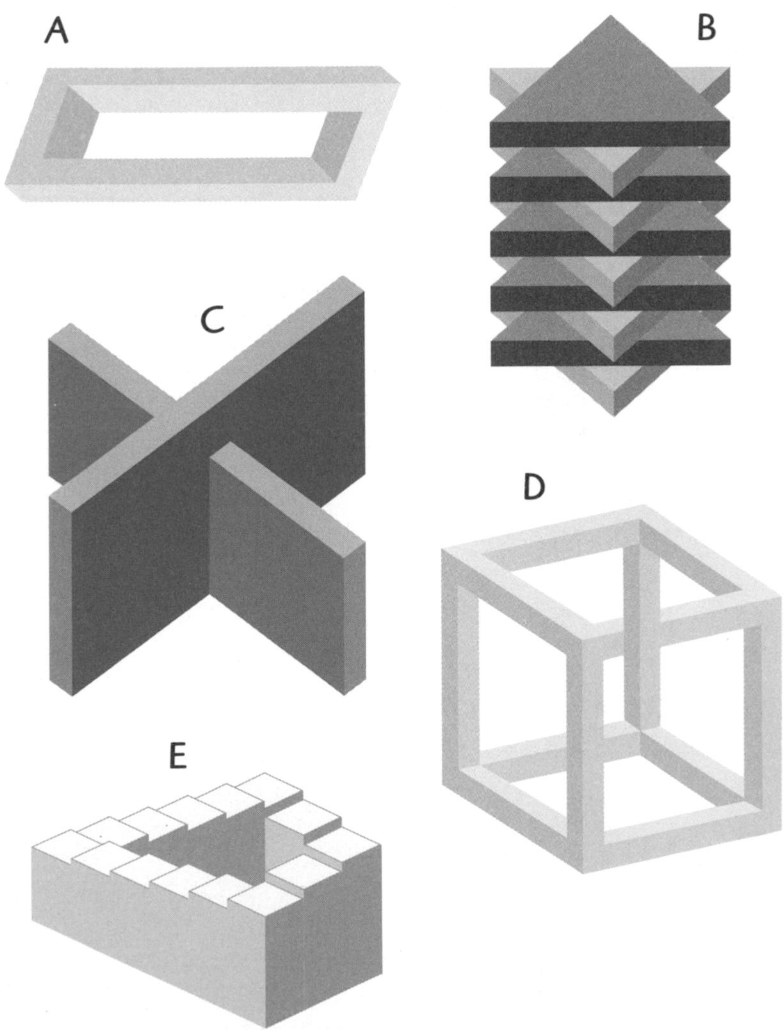

Tile pattern

See if you can complete this grid by discovering which is the missing block.

A

B

C

Salon selection

Minna has moved to a small, remote island. She wants to get her hair cut, and there are two stylists to choose from. One works in a modern salon and has an elegant bob of smooth brown hair. The other works in a wooden shack and has a badly-dyed disaster of a haircut. Which stylist should Minna choose?

Answer: ....

....

Square-eyed

Look at the pattern below. The blue square forms new squares as it fits around the red square. Then the yellow square fits around the blue square. How many squares are there in total?

1. ....

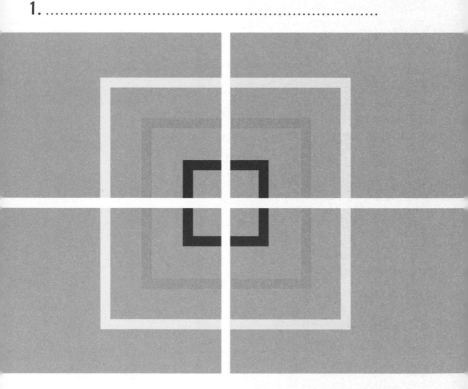

If a larger square were drawn around the yellow square, and an even larger square were drawn around that, how many squares would there be in the new pattern?

2. ....

Symbol scramble

Look for the pattern that follows from row to row.
Which three symbols are in the wrong position?

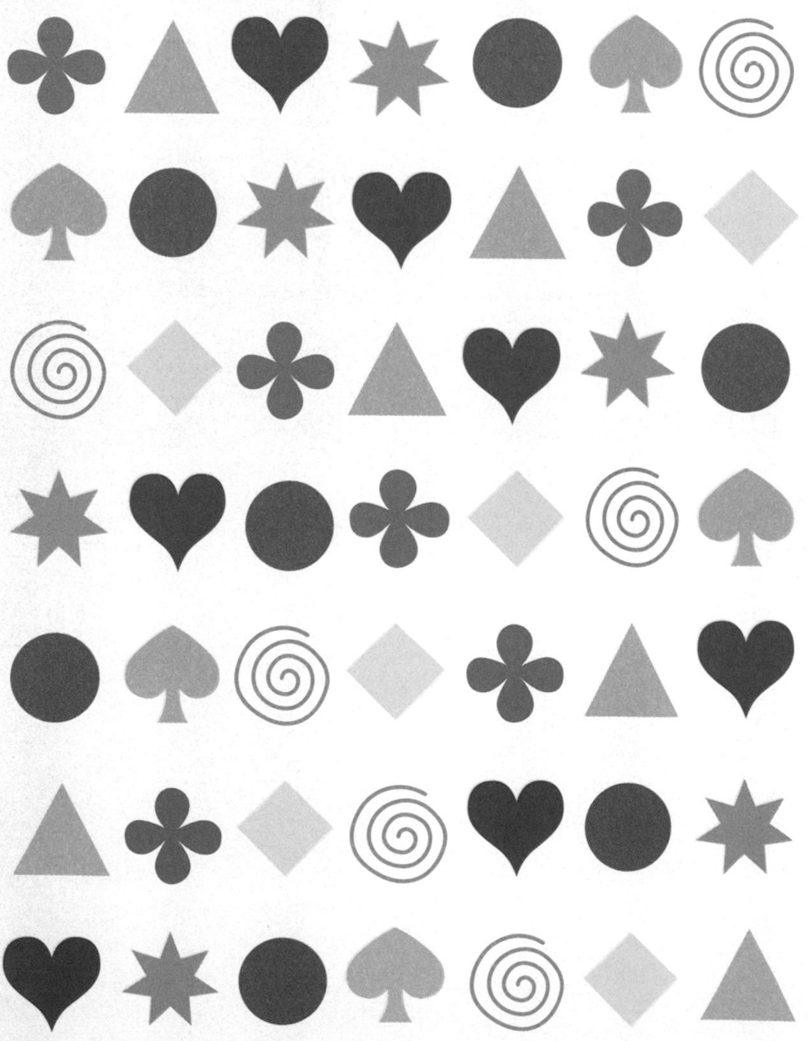

Dotty problem

These four dice show which number is on which side if a dice is rotated while keeping the '3' on top.

Now the dice are flipped so the '3' is at the bottom, and '4' is on top. Can you fill in the missing dots?

Castle code

The symbols on shields 1, 2 and 3 are related to their castles. Find out how, and draw the correct symbols on shield 4.

Laundry line-up

Look carefully for the sequence on this line, and decide which collection of laundry should be hung up next.

Cube in a cube

Which small cube completes the large cube?

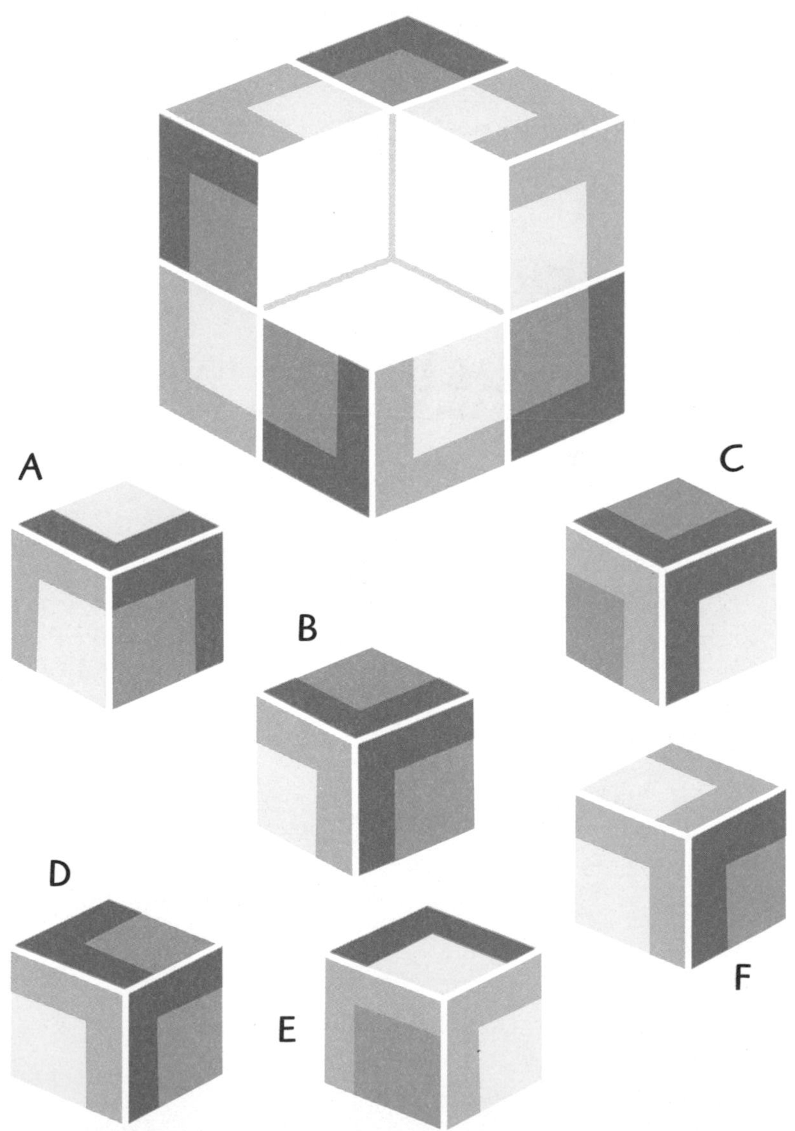

Keep it simple!

See if you can find the hidden message on the wall.

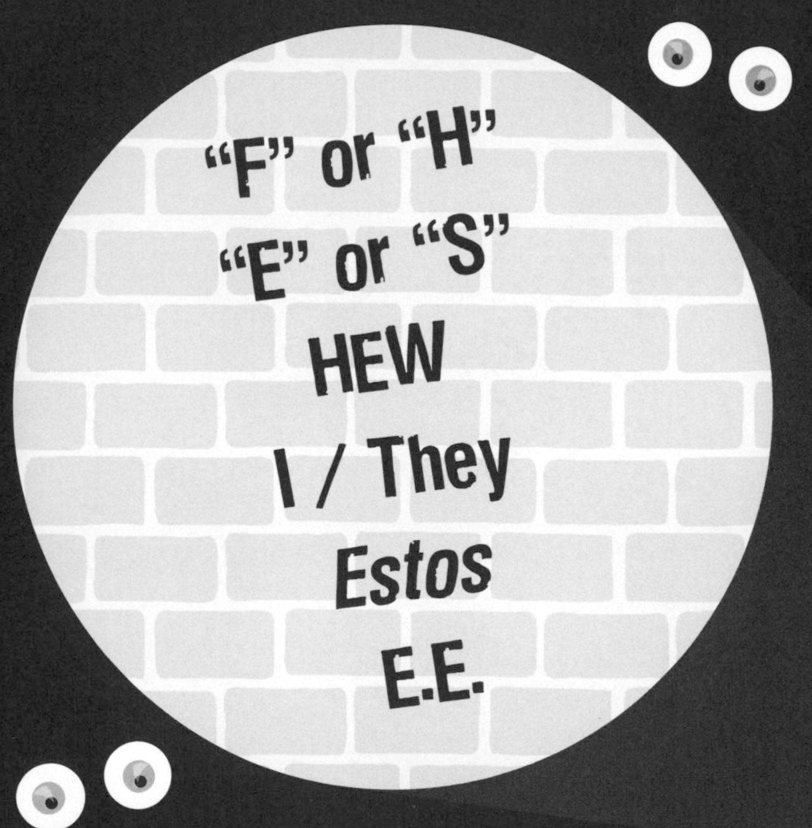

Answer: ....

....

Act your age

1. On her birthday, William asks his great aunt Millicent how old she is, and she replies: "Well, young man, I am 44 years old, not counting Saturdays, Sundays or Mondays, because I hate Mondays." What is her real age?

Answer: ....

2. William copies his great aunt's idea, but changes it to make himself sound older than he really is. He calculates his age in nine-day weeks, because he'd like his weekends to be twice as long. If his real age is 14, how old does he say he is?

Answer: ....

Arctic explorers

Three explorers are setting out on an Arctic trek. Following the clues on the opposite page, find out the age of each explorer and what food and drink they each pack in their backpacks.

Name	Age	Drink	Food
Ernest			
Roald			
Robert			

1. The man who packs the *cocoa* and smoked fish is younger than Robert.

2. The man who packs the *coffee*, but not the baked beans, is 27 years *old*.

3. Roald is 31 years *old*.

4. Ernest didn't pack the tea.

You can use the chart below to keep track of the facts.

	27	31	34	Coffee	Tea	Cocoa	Beef	Fish	Beans
Robert									
Ernest									
Roald									
Beef									
Fish									
Beans									
Coffee									
Tea									
Cocoa									

Boat crossing

A ferry sets out from Dublin for Liverpool. At the same time, a speedboat sets out from Liverpool for Dublin. If the ferry goes at 20 knots and the speedboat goes at 40 knots, which boat is closer to Dublin when they pass?

Answer: ....

90

Easy peasy

This is a most unusual paragraph. How quickly can you find out what's so unusual about it? It looks so ordinary you'd think nothing was wrong with it – and in fact, nothing is wrong with it. It is unusual though. Why? Study it, think about it, and you'll soon find out. You can do it without coaching, don't worry! Just stay calm and it'll dawn on you. Good luck.

M
O
N A
U G S I

Answer: ....

Robot shootout

Three robots are having a shootout: Spike, Razor and Glitch. Their stun guns each have one shot. Glitch is the most accurate, but Spike is quickest on the draw and gets to shoot first. What should he do to have the best chance of surviving?

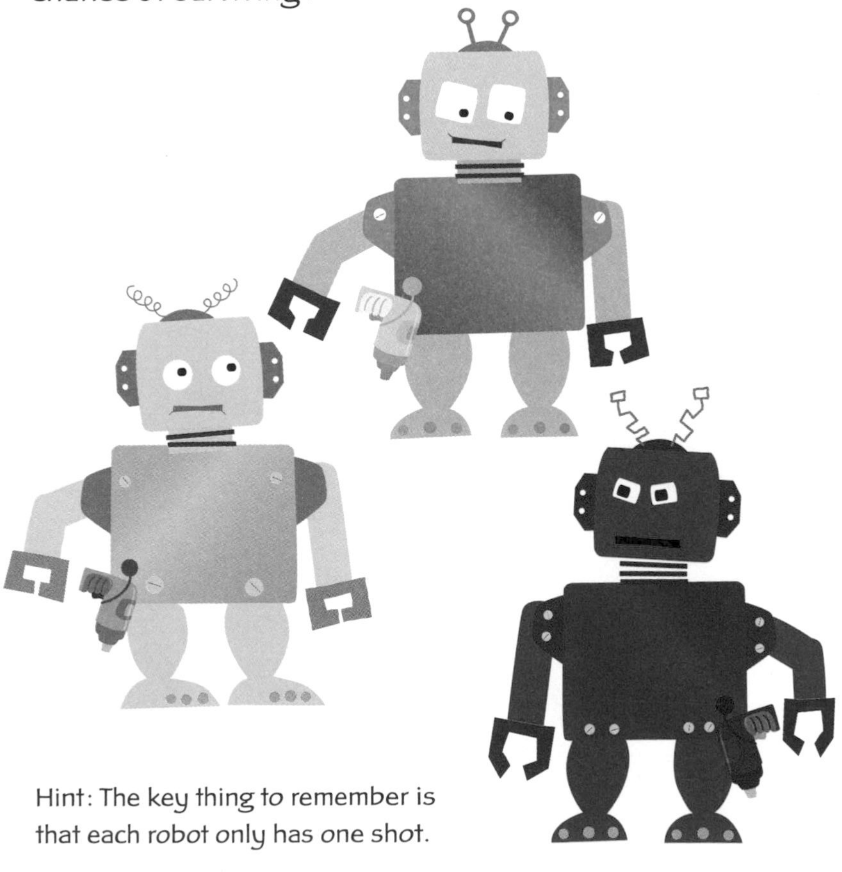

Hint: The key thing to remember is that each robot only has one shot.

a) shoot Glitch   b) shoot Razor   c) deliberately miss

Dolls' parade

Can you move just three of these dolls so that the triangle points down instead of up?

Monster munch

There are five monsters living under Tom's bed. "Feed us cookies!" they howl. "Or we'll gobble you up!" Luckily, they're not as fierce as they sound. The biggest monster sticks out a furry hand, and asks for half of the cookies on Tom's plate. Then it gives one cookie back as a thank-you present. The second-biggest monster does the same thing, then the third, the fourth, and the fifth.

If Tom wants to save two cookies for a midnight snack, what's the fewest number of cookies he can take to bed?

Hint: it's fewer than you think...

Answer: ....

Bridge crossing

Sally has to cross a rope bridge, but she's very nervous. The bridge has 20 planks, and every time she steps forwards five planks, she then steps backwards four planks. How many times must she do this to reach the other side?

Answer: ....

Non-stop pen

Draw these shapes without lifting your pen from the page or going over any line that you've already made.

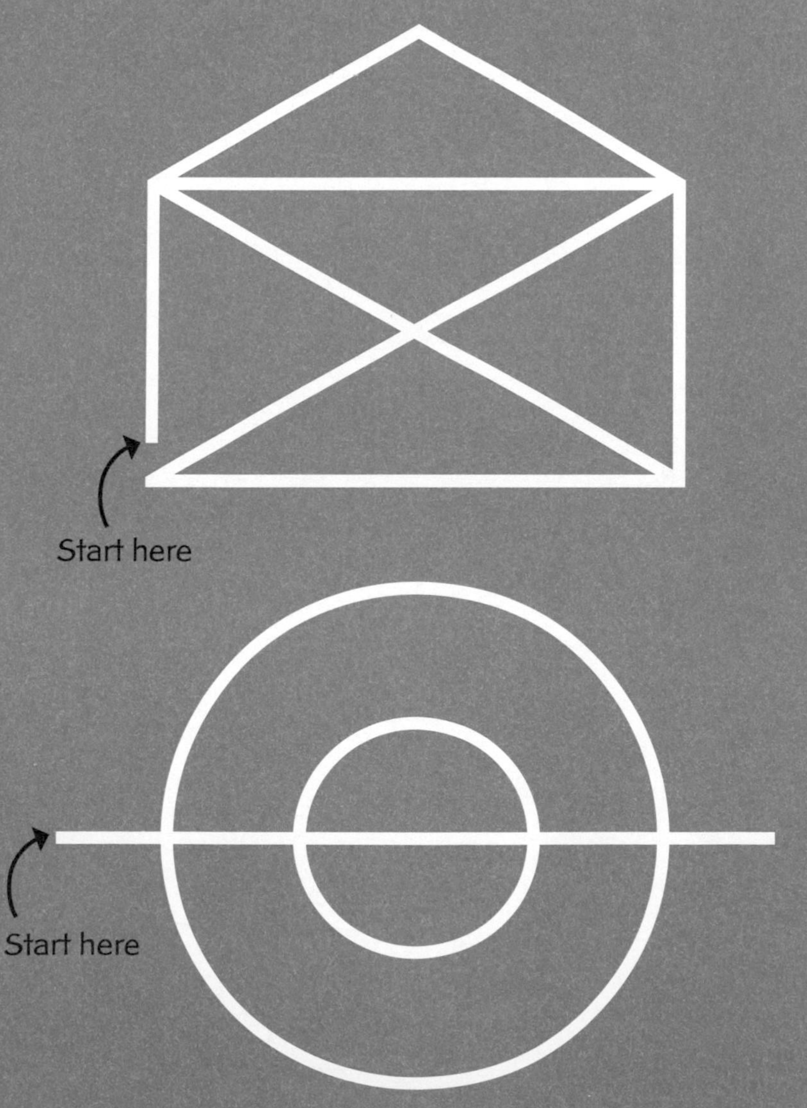

On and off

There are three light switches outside a room, and three lightbulbs on the inside. The switches are turned off and the door is closed. You can turn each switch on and off, but only before you open the door. How can you tell which switch controls which bulb when you enter the room?

Hint: There's more than one way to tell if a bulb has been on...

Answer: ....

....

Hard evidence

In each set of statements, underline the **two** which prove that:

1. Billy didn't rob the bank.

a. Billy said he didn't rob the bank.
b. Billy works at a supermarket in the morning.
c. The getaway driver is Billy's brother.
d. The bank was robbed at 10am.
e. Billy robbed a bank ten years ago.

2. Cathy has eaten a slice of her mother's cake.

a. A slice of cake is missing.
b. Cathy's mother bakes delicious cakes.
c. Cathy has a sweet tooth.
d. The cake was covered in chocolate.
e. Cathy has cake crumbs around her lips.

3. Simon is a werewolf.

a. Simon has very hairy arms.
b. A werewolf ate a yellow canary.
c. Simon never goes out on a full moon.
d. A werewolf was seen near Simon's house.
e. Simon has yellow feathers stuck between his teeth.

Apples and oranges

There are three boxes, one filled with apples, one with oranges and one with apples and oranges. But every box is mislabelled. You can pick a box and take one piece of fruit without looking inside. Which one should you choose to find out exactly what's in each box?

Hint: Which box can have only one type of fruit inside?

Answer:..

Alien code

An alien civilization uses number symbols made from dots and wavy lines. Some of them are shown below. Can you fill in the missing symbols?

0 1 2 3 4

5 6 7 8 9

10 11 12 13 14

15 16 17 18 19

Little riddlers

Riddle 1. Alesha and her friends are walking across the park on a bright, sunny day. Suddenly they find an old brown hat, a green scarf and some lumps of coal lying on the ground. Why are they not surprised?

Riddle 2. If two people can paint two rooms in two days, how long does it take one person to paint one room?

Riddle 3. There are five lollipops inside a paper bag. How can you give five people a lollipop each, and still have one left inside the bag?

Riddle 4. Every day, trains travel between Trumpington and Gravelly Bottom. They travel on the same track, at the same speed, and there are no stations in between. The 1pm train took 70 minutes to complete the trip, but the 3pm train took an hour and ten minutes. Why?

Riddle 5. How could a cowboy ride into town on Friday, stay three days, and then ride out on Friday?

Answers

1. Boat race

Three

2. Lost stone

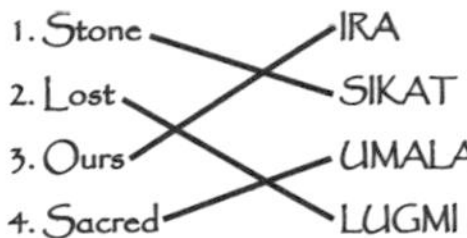

3. Odd one out

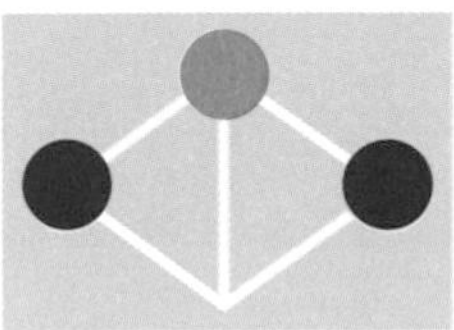

4. Alien weigh-in

1. 40 grobbles. The baby alien's whole weight is made from half its weight, plus 20 grobbles. Therefore those 20 grobbles must be the other half of the whole.
2. 80 grobbles (same logic)

5. Tricky traffic

Car 2 on Wood Lane. All the cars have two windows and purple hubcaps.
Car 3 on Castle Road. All the cars have three windows and hubcaps that match their paint.

6. Toy cube

D

7. Dotty squares

3 dots.
Across: 4+3 = 7, 3+1 = 4, 1+2 = 3
Down: 4–3 = 1, 3–1 = 2, 7–4 = 3

8. Who lives where?

1. Andy and Rose
2. Ray and Mia
3. Mike and Anna

9. Bus driver riddle

He was walking.

10. The jump

She jumped out of a window on the bottom floor.

11. Racing positions

Blue - 1st Yellow - 2nd
Purple - 3rd Red - 4th
Green - 5th

12. Pen puzzle

Answers

13. Shapes and numbers

24

Count the number of sides and multiply by four.

14. Which kitten?

Friend	Kitten
Zack	Tiger
Ellie	Shadow
Amy	Rusty
Rico	Sooty

15. Fishy puzzle

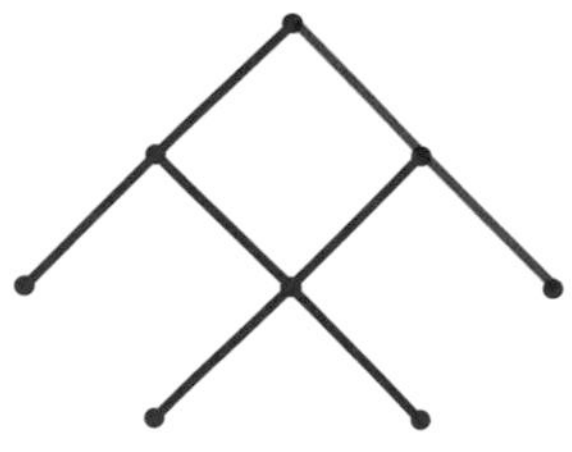

16. Odd pattern out

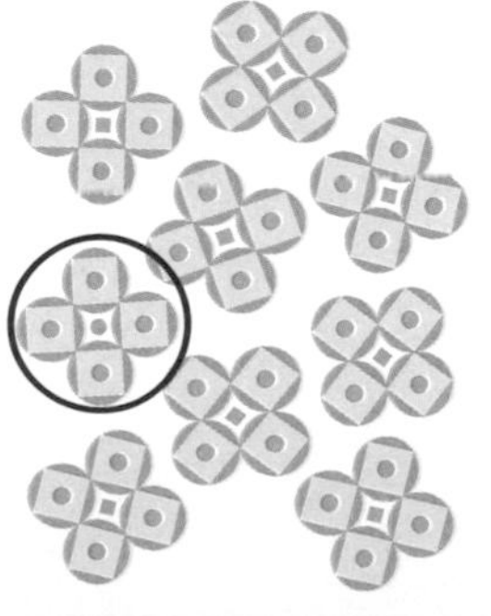

17. Dog toys

	Jojo	Rex	Spot	Bone	Ball	Stick
Ali		✓				✓
Pat			✓	✓		
Riz	✓				✓	

18. Pencil puzzle

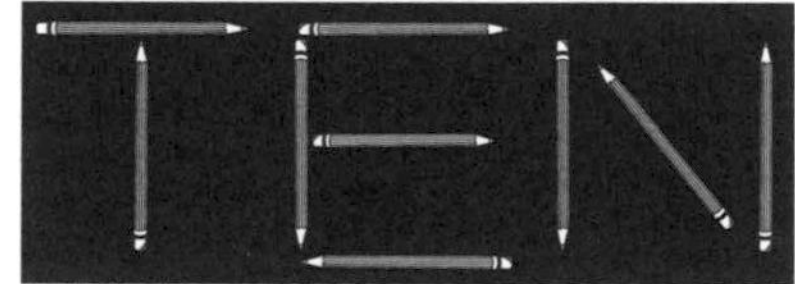

19. The wise son

The younger son rode his brother's horse over the line.

20. Puzzle time

Their hands don't make a right angle (90°).

21. Dots on dice

Answers

22. Sudoku

6	9	1	2	7	3	8	5	4
8	4	3	1	5	6	9	2	7
5	2	7	9	8	4	1	3	6
4	6	2	7	9	1	3	8	5
1	5	9	6	3	8	4	7	2
3	7	8	5	4	2	6	1	9
2	8	6	4	1	5	7	9	3
7	1	4	3	2	9	5	6	8
9	3	5	8	6	7	2	4	1

23. Bell ringer

Around to the right. Where the cogs are touching, they turn in opposite directions. Cogs that are connected by a belt turn in the same direction.

24. Breakfast code

A. fried egg

F. two slices of toast

25. Mission to Mars

c) week 11. The total distance the rocket has covered doubles each week. Therefore the week before it arrives on Mars it will be halfway there.

26. Not knots

C

27. Genie's riddle

The third room (the lions would all be dead).

28. Right rectangle

C

Each segment is divided in half vertically.

29. Sequence challenge

3113112221 1 A.

Each line describes the line above. For example, '1 A' is described as '1 1 1 A' because you say: "one 1 and one A".

30. Follow the cogs

Right

Touching cogs turn in opposite directions.

D

Answers

31. Fish in a bowl

B. The fish facing left in the first bowl disappear, and the ones facing right turn around and face left.

32. Hen names

Henny 2, Po 6, Maisie 3, Meg 1, Gina 4, Eggwina 5. The number of letters in their name matches the number of feathers on their wing.

33. Block prints

C

34. Detective school

4. It's the only statement telling the truth about the number of other statements that are false.

35. Cake gobbler

C. The bites on the round cake go around to the right. The bites on the oblong cake go around to the left.

36. Wild West

Day	Cowboy	Horse	Errand
Thursday	Butch	Betsy	Saddle
Friday	Jesse	Dusty	Debt
Saturday	Billy	Red Lady	Dentist

37. Pencils and pens

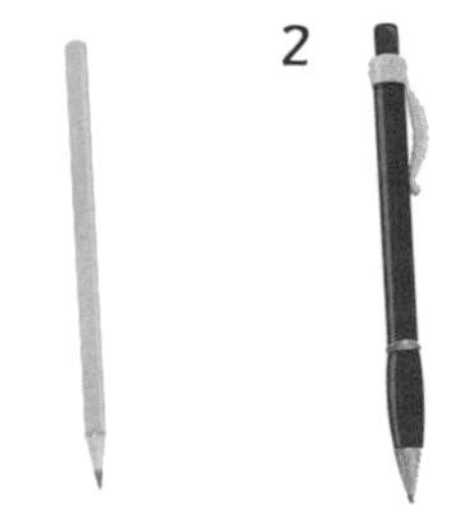

38. Shooting stars

A and F

39. Cuckoo clock

Four seconds. It takes two seconds between each strike.

40. Murder mystery

The wife. Dalla can't be right, because if she is, then Lou would also be right. Since Dalia is wrong, then Sam is wrong, too. That means Anil is correct.

Answers

41. Patchwork pattern

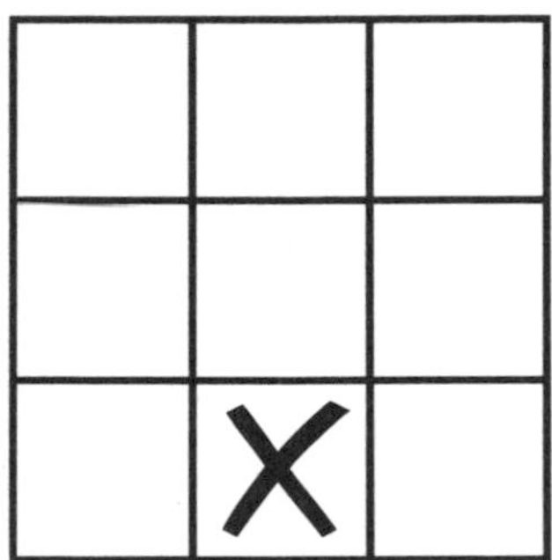

A different square changes places with the middle each time. In square 2, the top middle changes. In square 3, the top right changes. And so on, in a clockwise direction.

42. Prism picker

B, C and F

43. Postage puzzle

32 (top middle)
23 (top right)
33 (middle left)
12 (middle right)
The first number matches the number of butterflies, the second number relates to the background of each stamp.

44. Puzzling print

C

45. See-saw scales

The ball weighs the same as three triangles. The square weighs the same as two triangles.

46. Jester's riddle

Three daughters. One blonde, one brunette, one with red hair.

47. Near miss

He's in a tunnel, or on a bridge.

48. Shape shifter

A

49. Roman riddle

b) three. The password is the number of letters in whatever number the guard says.

Answers

50. Cryptic grid

51. Symbol sudoku

52. Pattern puzzler

c

53. Tom the cat

Peasant: 4 years
Ship: 2 years
Sultan: 8 years
Age: 16 years old

Add the fractions to get $\frac{7}{8}$. That means the 2 years he's spent in the mayor's house are the other $\frac{1}{8}$. From this you can work out how many years each fraction represents.

54. Detective work

1. b and d
2. a and e
3. c and e

55. Seaside puzzle

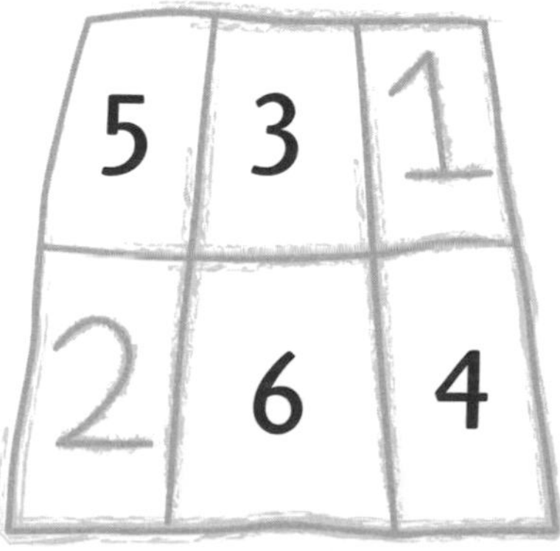

Answers

56. Choose carefully

"Which door would the OTHER guard say the treasure is behind?"
It doesn't matter which guard she asks; the answer is always a lie. The lying guard would tell her a lie. The honest guard would tell her what the liar would say, which would be the same lie. So the treasure is always behind the opposite door.

57. Testing tubes

a) 4 hrs and 5 mins.
It would take five minutes of heating to go from one test tube of mixture to two.

58. Art club

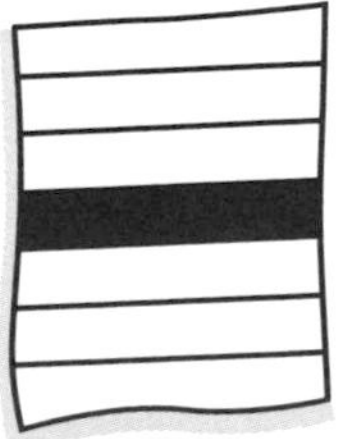

The first picture shows halves, the second shows thirds, the third shows quarters, and so on.

59. Hat puzzler

B. A doesn't shout out, so he must see two different hats. Therefore B knows his hat is not the same as C's.

60. Lollipop pick

B. The lollipops move one place to the right, and the last one becomes the first.

61. Pattern streamers

The streamers follow the sequence 1, 2, 3, 4, 5 ; 2, 3, 4, 5, 1 ; 3, 4, 5, 1, 2, and so on.

62. Planes puzzle

Day 12. 12 is the first number that can be divided exactly by 1, 2, 3 and 4 days.

	1	2	3	4
Day 1	x			
Day 2	x	x		
Day 3	x		x	
Day 4	x	x		x
Day 5	x			
Day 6	x	x	x	
Day 7	x			
Day 8	x	x		x
Day 9	x		x	
Day 10	x	x		
Day 11	x			
Day 12	x	x	x	x

Answers

63. Faulty calculator

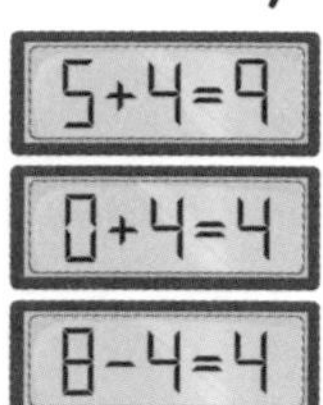

64. River crossing

Left shore	On the boat	Right shore
F,R,C		
F,C	R	
F,C		R
C	F	R
C	R	F
R	C	F
R		F, C
	R	F, C
		R,F,C

First you take the rabbit across. Then you take the fox across and bring back the rabbit. Then you take the carrot across and leave it with the fox. Finally, you take the rabbit across.

65. Sudoku

8	3	9	4	7	6	5	1	2
7	2	4	1	3	5	9	6	8
1	6	5	9	8	2	7	4	3
3	5	7	8	6	4	2	9	1
9	1	6	2	5	7	3	8	4
2	4	8	3	1	9	6	7	5
4	7	3	6	2	1	8	5	9
5	9	2	7	4	8	1	3	6
6	8	1	5	9	3	4	2	7

66. Paperboy puzzle

48. The next house number is always double the one before.

67. Cube finder

B

68. Wrong total

24 doesn't divide equally by seven.

69. Age puzzler

Laura is 30. (Her mother is 60.)

70. Tricky triangles

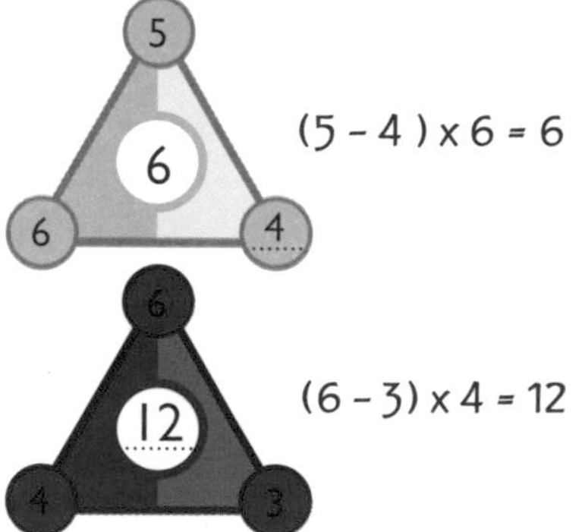

71. In the bay

Name	Owner	Number	Age
Salt Spray	Mick	364	1 year
Merrimack	Joss	109	3 years
Crab's Claw	Seb	238	2 years

Answers

72. What's the time?

1 o'clock. The sequence is +2, +3, +2, and so on.

73. Bird's eye view

C

74. Short puzzles

1. E, for Eight. The sequence goes One, Two, Three, Four...
2. WHITE
3. Mary
4. 0% (It will be midnight.)

75. Parrot in a cage

Cage = 5 silver pieces
Parrot = 45 silver pieces

76. Jumbo jumble

Weigh two elephants from different pairs. If one weighs more than the other, it must be from the heavier pair; if they weigh the same, the elephants from the other pair must be heavier.

77. Impossible shapes

A, D, E

78. Tile pattern

A. Each row and column contains one stick of each size, one red oval and one green oval.

79. Salon selection

The stylist who works in the wooden shack. There are only two stylists on the island, so they must cut each other's hair. Therefore, the one with the worse haircut must be the better stylist.

80. Square-eyed

1. 15
2. 25

Each large square adds five new squares to the pattern.

81. Symbol scramble

The sequence is eight symbols long and snakes downwards from the top left corner.

Answers

82. Dotty problem

83. Castle code

The bars represent the windows and the arrow represents the type of door.

84. Laundry line-up

C. The pegs are in sequence.

85. Cube in a cube

B

86. Keep it simple!

'For he or she with eyes to see'. Ignore all the punctuation and styles, just write the letters out in a line.

87. Act your age

1. 77. She is only counting $\frac{4}{7}$ of her age. To find her true age, divide her false age by 4 and multiply by 7.
2. 18. He is counting $\frac{9}{7}$ of his age. To find this fake age, divide his real age by 7 and multiply by 9.

88. Arctic explorers

Name	Age	Drink	Food
Ernest	27	Coffee	Beef
Roald	31	Cocoa	Fish
Robert	34	Tea	Beans

89. Boat crossing

They'll both be exactly the same distance from Dublin as they pass each other.

90. Easy peasy

The whole paragraph doesn't contain a single 'e', even though it's the most common letter in the English language.

Answers

91. Robot shootout

c) deliberately miss. Whichever robot he shoots, the other robot will then shoot him. But if he misses he's no longer a threat. Then the robot who fires next will shoot the third robot. This leaves two robots standing, but no shots left.

92. Dolls' parade

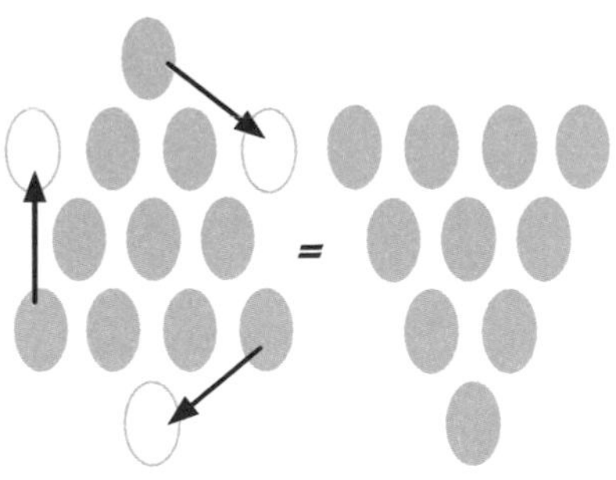

93. Monster munch

Two cookies. Every time Tom gives a monster half of his cookies (one cookie), the monster gives it back.

94. Bridge crossing

16. On the 16th time she steps off the bridge, so she doesn't step backwards.

95. Non-stop pen

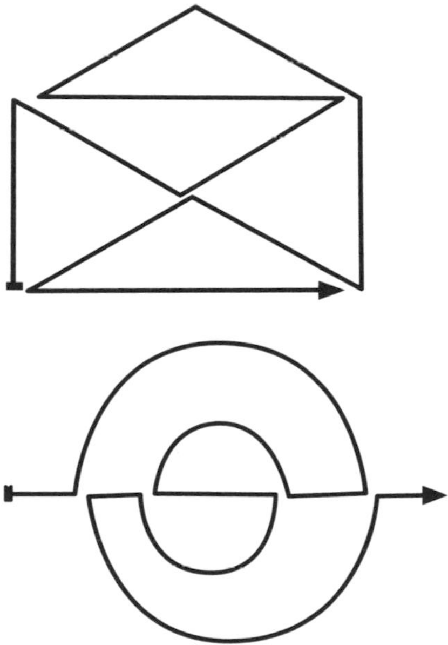

96. On and off

Turn two switches on, then turn one off after about thirty seconds. When you walk into the room, two lightbulbs will be off, but one will still be warm.

97. Hard evidence

1. b and d
2. a and e
3. b and e

Answers

98. Apples and oranges

The box labelled "apples and oranges". All the labels are wrong, so this is the only box that can't contain both apples and oranges. Once you know which fruit it does contain, you can easily work out the other two boxes by remembering their labels are wrong too.

99. Alien code

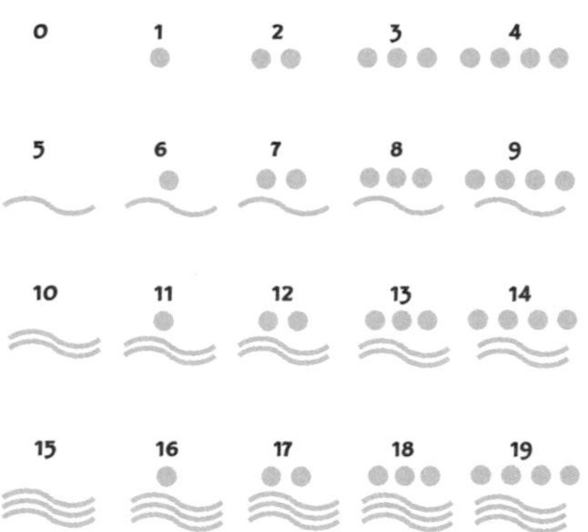

100. Little riddlers

1. The hat, scarf and lumps of coal were part of a snowman that melted because it was a warm day.

2. Two days

3. When you give out the last lollipop, give it inside the bag.

4. An hour and ten minutes is the same as 70 minutes.

5. Friday is the name of his horse.

Written by Simon Tudhope. Designed by Marc Maynard and Ruth Russell. Illustrated by Lizzie Barber and Non Figg.

First published in 2014 by Usborne Publishing Ltd. 83–85 Saffron Hill, London ECIN 8RT, England. UE. First published in America in 2016.